1 MONTH OF
FREE
READING

at

www.ForgottenBooks.com

By purchasing this book you are eligible for one month membership to ForgottenBooks.com, giving you unlimited access to our entire collection of over 1,000,000 titles via our web site and mobile apps.

To claim your free month visit: www.forgottenbooks.com/free896658

ISBN 978-0-265-83597-5
PIBN 10896658

This book is a reproduction of an important historical work. Forgotten Books uses
state-of-the-art technology to digitally reconstruct the work, preserving the original format
whilst repairing imperfections present in the aged copy. In rare cases, an imperfection in
the original, such as a blemish or missing page, may be replicated in our edition. We do,
however, repair the vast majority of imperfections successfully; any imperfections that
remain are intentionally left to preserve the state of such historical works.

For support please visit www.forgottenbooks.com

Mr. Marbois came to my lodgings & appointments of Mr.
Livingston, at the other. & and I being indisposed
it was agreed that I might repose as it suited me.
Mr. Livingston opened the conversation by presenting
us with the project of the gov.t to be proposed to us,
which he admitted he thought hard and unreason-
able; he presented at the same time another project wh
he called his own, & which had not been seen by the
gov.t, & but to which he presumed the first consul was
assent, as he had told him he could not insist on the terms
contained in the words; and could only ask or propose
such as he had drawn in the second; but to which
he declared that the first consul had not assented
explicitly. Mr. Marbois thought himself however at
liberty to propose his own project as the basis of
of our negotiation. That project claimed ----
& the debt due our citizens estimated at 20. more.
His own reduced that demand to 50, including the
debt. There were some other differences between
them, his going more into detail, in the form of
a ---- particular act. Mr. Livingston observed that the debt was a thing to be provided for
in an official manner; that the consul had said to
him it sho.d be paid; that we ought to begin from pts
agreed & proceed to difficulties - that the points agreed

were the debts that were due and our right of deposit.
Mr. Marbois said that if we made a treaty on the gen-
l great subject of the Louisiana, he wod. include in it a
provision for the debts; that if he did not make a
a treaty of that kind he wod. leave nothing to do with
the ~~treaty~~ debts. Mr. Livingston repeated the promise
of the Consul &ca for the payment of them, to which
Mr. Marbois replied that he did not mean to im-
pair the force of our claim founded on the treaty
& the promise of the govt. – what he meant to say
was, that if our negotiation succeeded in the object
of it, the debts wod. be comprized in it & provided
for, and if it did not succeed, he wod. leave them
where he found them; they claim wod. still be supported
by the treaty & any assurance Mr. Livingston may
have recd. from the govt. since. Mr. Livingston
still pressing the high ground on wh. the claim to
the paymt. of the debt rested, Mr. Marbois observing
that in the promise referr'd to no time was fixd.
or sum specified, & intimated that the Consul did
not contemplate a greater sum than 3 or 4. millions of livres. I then observed that I thought we
were all of the same opinion respecting the debts,
that the ground on wh. they stood wod. not be impaird
by the failure of this negotiation; that ~~the~~ a provision might be made for the payment of them by it,
that we had better go on to the ~~that obj.d~~ with that view, to
examine & discuss the
project presented by Mr. Marbois. One of the articles
contained in Mr. Marbois's project, proposed that

& the French govt.

the payment to our citizens shod. proceed in equal
degree regarding the amt. to be paid to each party,
by the month; that is that ~~~~ neither shod. have
a priority or preference to the other. as to time
or proportion. Mr. Livingston insisted that the payment to our citizens shod. be prompt & full, which he
supposed we might make, without ~~~~ rendering
ourselves unable to meet the views of the French
govt. in any sum we might stipulate to give in
point of time: to that Mr. Marbois seemed to
have no objection. ^

my colleague wrote Mr. ~~~~ Marbois's project
with him & took ~~~~ one very loosely & improperly drawn
which with our communications ~~~~ together on the subject &
the modifications we gave it, will be noted hereafter

we called on Mr. Marbois the 29th and gave
him our project which we read to him &
discussed. we ~~~~ proposed to offer 50. millions
to France & 20. on acct. of her debt to the ~~~~ citizens of the
US States,
making 70. in the whole. on reading this art. he declared that he wod. not proceed in the negotiation on
a less sum than 80. millions, since it wod. be useless as
the consul had been sufficiently explicit on that point.
government.
indeed he assured us that his head never been posi:
instructed him
tively ~~~~ to take that sum, but that he
and told the consul ~~~~ it was enough, that ~~~~ wod. no more, and for ~~~~
~~~~ he ~~~~ to take it; ~~~~
~~~~ he was ~~~~, he Mr. Marbois had thought himself cautious)
to accept & propose it to us, but that he wod. not proceed unless we ~~~~

agreed to give it on this branch & explicitly declared on his views. &

after explaining to him the motive which led us to ~~make the offer~~ that sum ~~we agreed to accede to his~~ idea a ~~offer~~ give 80 millions, he asked us if we wd. not advance something immediately, we replied, we did so in discharge of their debt to our citizens, they they had suffered and it was for the interest of ~~them~~ as well as the US labor that they shod. be promptly paid, or as soon as possible. To the payment .. stock, we did not object, nor did he say any thing respecting the ~~loss~~ to be sustained by it: he asked wt. effect the protracting the redemption of the stock for 15 years wod. have on its value; we told him to raise its price.

On the proviso to the commercial stipulation he seemed to entertain a doubt, but on our shewing the abuse of wh. the article was capable with out it, being not simply to ~~give~~ a preference & manufacturers for 12 years to French vessels over those of oth. countries in the ports of the ceded territory, but to ~~enable~~ France to monopolize the carrying of the exports from the mississippi, and ~~exclude~~ a single article raised there being bot. from the other states, such as tobacco vice &c, he ~~seemed to~~ admitted that such a power was not sought on this part.

He seemed desirous to secure by some strong provision the incorporation of the inha: bitants of the ceded country with our union; we told him that we wod. try to modify the ar : ticle to meet his idea, as fully as we cod. – we left our project with him, in expectation of hearing from him soon the result, as he said he shoud see the consul next morning on the subject. He informd me that Mr. Talleyrand had asked him whether I was in health to be presented to the first consul, & on my answering in the affirmative; advised me to let him know it. My colleague promised as we returned home to inform the minister that I had recovered my health, next day. To guard against accidents however I wrote the minister to that effect next morning, and a note to my colleague to request him to call for me as he went to the house of the minister. Just as I was ready to visit the minister my colleague returned from him, & informed me that it was arranged that I shoud be presented next day, that is on the first of may.

May 1st Sunday.

; accompanied my colleague to the Palace of the powers, where I was presented by him to the consul; while standing in the circle I recievd a communication by the prefect of the palace from the minister stating that he was indisposed, but that I must present the consul my letter of credence, & that the consul desired I woud dine with him.

When the consul came round to me, mr. Livingston presented me to him, on which the

consul observed that he was glad to see me; I was
bien aise de le vois. you have been here 15. days
I told him I had - "you speak french" I replied
"a little." "you had a good voyage", "yes". "You came
in a frigate" no, in a merchant vessel chosen
for the purpose " col: Mercer was presented; says he
he is secy of legation " no but my friend". He then
made enquiries of mr. Livingston & his secy. how
their families were; and then turned to Mr. Livings=
ton & myself & observed that our affrs stood all
settled.

We dined with him. After dinner the first
when we retired into the saloon, the first
consul came up to me and asked whether the federal
city grew much, I told him it did: How many in
habitants has it? It is just commencing, there are
two cities near it, one above, the other below, on the
same great river Potowk, which if united would make
a respectable town, in itself it contains only two or
three thousand inhabitants. well; Mr. Jefferson, how
old is he abt sixty. Is he married or single; he is not
married - then he is a garçon, no he is a widower; has
he children? yes who are they two daughters married; does he reside
always at the fedl city, yes young, generally. are
the publick buildings there commodious, then for
the congress & President especially? they are. You the
americans did brilliant things in yr war with En
=gland, you will do the same again. I am
persuaded always believe well when it shall be

419

our lot to be in war. You may probably be in war
with them again. I replied I did not know, that that
was an important question to decide when there would
be an occasion for it.

at ½ after eight we met Mr. Marbois at his own
lodging, in conformity to an appointment which we
made with him & the Consuls, and entered on the subject of our proposed treaty. He objected to the first art.
as being very & unnecessary superfluities, & thought a
mark to that effect on it by the department of foreign
affairs, as being an act more suited to a private transac-
tion before a notary publick. Objected also to any guarantie
as agst France or Spn as agst France as useless, since
the assive was as strong a guarranty agst her as the
tel. maker, and agst Spn it improper & useless since it wod be an
ungracious act to her from France, & we had nothing
to fear from Spain. He had no objection to inserting the
art. of the treaty of Ildefonso by which France acquired the territory, in our treaty, & wod engage her
good offices with Spain in support of our claim to
the Floridas.   From the 2d art: he agreed to strike
out whatever restricted the application of publick bring
ing in the same war hereafter; & to be contented with the
security of property to individuals; and also to omit
the obligation to transfer the archives due to the local
authorities. The art. at the close of our project which
respected the upon & transfer of the territory, he
proposed to put together for the commencement, which
we examined & modified somewhat by consent,

450

that which respected the commerce particularly, he said was objected to in the proviso; he admitted however more than an exemption from foreign duties in the introduction of the same into the ports of the mississippi but not to affect the terms on wh. our produce shod be carried from it, since he readily foresaw that such a power might be greatly abused. I proposed an amendment which was in sentiment agreed to, the stock to be paid them, and the mode by which we proposed to ascertain the amt. and also the persons entitled to the debt they owed over citizens, he said objections were entertained. they wish the payment to be made here of 5. millions of livres the month, wh. we told him was impossible — he believed it was. He wished the term for which the stock was irredeemable to be omitted & adjusted afterward between ourselves, intimating that we on that point difficulties existed with his gov't. we proved it from want of time to examine it, but that we must agree on something, and he seemed to assent particularly to our ideas on the subject. on our explaining the reasons why some check on the liquidation of the debt due our citizens was necessary, since otherwise the sum destined to them might be absorbed, by liquidations in favor of americans not entitled, or even persons not americans, he admitted the propriety of the check we proposed. He said he wod. see the Consul next morning, fix the points in question, & come prepared the day to conclude & sign the treaty as we saw of yesterday, being saturday.

421

may 2d was actually signed the treaty and convention
for the sixty millions of francs to France in french
language, but our copies in English not being ready out
we cod. not sign in our language. They were however
prepared & signed in two or three days afterward. The
convention respecting American claims was took more
time & was not signed till about the 8. or 9th. was a more
minute view of this business as promised in the 3d. page will
be annexed hereafter.

We nominated provisionally Ld. John Mercer
I. C. Barnett & Wm. McClure to examine the claims
of americans on the french govt. and performing the duties assigned to us
bd. by the convention respecting that subject.

As soon as we had dispatched the treaty &ca by
Mr. Hughes, with duplicates & triplicates, I resolved
to go to Spn. in pursuit of my instructions, which
Mr. L. approved & strongly urged. with that view I
wrote a note to the minister of foreign affrs. asking
the good offices work of his govt. with Spn. as had
been promised by Mr. Marbois intimating that I
wished to set out in a few days for Madrid. On
the sunday following I dined with the consul
Lumbuzces, who arrived late from the coun-
cil at St. Cloud. The party was not large; I sat

422

next him; he observed "you must not go to spain at pre-
=sent". I asked his reason. He replied it is not the time,
but he declined going more into it. after dinner when
we were in the saloon, he came up to me, and on my
telling him that he had given me some uneasiness by what
he had said, he replied "it was only his opinion, but
you will talk on the subject with the minister of
the publick Treasury" [Mr Marbois] which I pro-
=mised. I went immediately to Mr Marbois's but
he was not at home. Reflecting on the hint from
the consul it occurr'd it not be proper to call on the
ambassador of spn. & confer with him on the
subject, as I had always intended before I sate out
for spn. I found him at home with two spanish
gentlemen, one the husband of the daughter of Don
Galvez who was also present. I told him that I intended go
up to spn. to treat for Florida with the minister of his
catholic majesty, & asked what he thought of it. He replied with great candor that he wished the affair a-
micably settled between our govts. & that two days before he had written to his court by an extraordinary courier at the de-
sire of Mr Livingston to propose to it
the question whether it would make the
upon and as I understood to authorise him to treat him
for it. As Mr Livingston had never spoken to me on the
subject, as he had proposed my going to spn., or at least give

215

his decided opinion that I ought to go there, this information sur-
prised me much, especially when I recollected that he had no power to treat on the subject, but knew that it was committed to
others. I asked when he expected an answer to his letter? He said
if it was sent by an extry courier it might be in 12. days, as
it required 7. to go and as many to return, & it had been
sent 2. already; that if it came by the ordinary post it
wo.d take much longer, it requiredp 12. days to convey
a letter from Paris to Madrid in that mode. I told him
that I thought I sho.d go, & then explained to him something
of the nature of the commn wh. existed for treating with his government, it being thought by ours more respectful to us to
treat at Madrid than here, but without giving cause to infer
that I disapproved the measure taken by Mr. Livingston or indd
that I was ignorant of it.

next day Mr. Livingston & myself called on Mr. Marbois on
some question relative to the treaty &c. on our return he asked
me when I sho.d set out to Spain? I told him that I had called
on the marquiss D'azara to confer with him on the subject
the night before, and of the step he had taken at his request to
draw the subject here; that under those circumstances it wo.d
be an idle errand for me to go there, till at least till the
marquiss got an answer to his letter; that the affr. ought not
to play between the two countries, he said that
what had passed between him and the marquiss had
happen'd casually, at the minister of foreign affs.; that
the marquiss had sent the extry. courier to announce our
treaty, & hearing him say he intended to send one,
he had suggested the idea of his proposing to his court
to make the offer, but not to obtain authority to treat
here for it. I told him that after the arrangement made
by our gov.t with respect to Spn., the affair ought to have its course in

the wagon in which it was plac'd lay it. that I could not see
any benefit to be derived from, the ambassador of Spain to his
court in the manner stated by mr. forsyth, especially if I was
to go there

LIBRARY OF CONGRESS.

PAPERS

OF

JAMES MONROE

LISTED IN CHRONOLOGICAL ORDER
FROM THE ORIGINAL MANUSCRIPTS
IN THE LIBRARY OF CONGRESS

COMPILED UNDER THE DIRECTION OF

WORTHINGTON CHAUNCEY FORD

CHIEF, DIVISION OF MANUSCRIPTS

WASHINGTON
GOVERNMENT PRINTING OFFICE
1904

PREFATORY NOTE

Under an Executive order issued by the President, March 9, 1903, the papers of James Monroe were transferred from the Department of State to the Library of Congress. These papers had been purchased by an act of Congress approved March 3, 1849. In 1893 the Department of State issued a calendar of them, the arrangement of which was alphabetical, the letters of Monroe being calendared separately from those of his correspondents. This alphabetical arrangement is convenient for determining the letters written by any one man; for historical purposes a chronological arrangement gives a better account of the sequence of the papers and develops the periods of political events. With this view the following list has been prepared, and by using it in connection with the calendar of the Department of State the student will be enabled to learn the contents of any particular paper mentioned in both list and calendar.

This list is not confined to such papers as come with the correspondence of Monroe under the Executive order, but includes such Monroe material as had been acquired by the Library of Congress. Two letter books (noted in the list by the letters L. B.) covering his service in the second French and first English missions, and a number of miscellaneous letters (noted by the letter M.) to be found in special collections have been listed. Intended, primarily, for the student of the history of this period, this list will also serve to show some of the resources of the Library of Congress in manuscript material for the years of Monroe's public service.

The "Journal" by Monroe of the negotiations which led to the cession of Louisiana is reproduced from the original manuscript.

The list was prepared by Mr. Wilmer Ross Leech, of the Division of Manuscripts.

WORTHINGTON CHAUNCEY FORD
Chief, Division of Manuscripts

HERBERT PUTNAM
Librarian of Congress
Washington, D. C., June 27, 1904

ILLUSTRATION

The most successful incident connected with Monroe's diplomatic expe-
rience was the visit to France in 1803, resulting in the purchase of the
Louisiana Territory. Much of the credit belongs to Robert R. Livingston,
who had conducted the preliminary negotiations, but Monroe felt that to
himself should be awarded the chief credit. The paper now reproduced
is entirely in Monroe's writing and is a rough diary of the events of the
days spent in the negotiations. It thus constitutes the best contemporary
account of his participation.

PAPERS OF JAMES MONROE

November	26.	John Tyler to Monroe.
	26.	Beverley Randolph to Monroe.
December	2.	John Marshall to Monroe.
	10.	Thomas Jefferson to Monroe.
	15.	Thomas Stone to Monroe.

1785.

January	14.	Thomas Jefferson to Monroe.
March	6.	Beverley Randolph to Monroe.
	11.	Joseph Jones to Monroe.
	18.	Thomas Jefferson to Monroe.
	18.	Thomas Stone to Monroe.
	—.	Thomas Jefferson to Monroe.
April	15.	" "
May	11.	
August	2.	James Tilton to Monroe.
October	17.	Richard Henry Lee to Monroe.
November	28.	William Grayson to Monroe.
December	11.	Thomas Jefferson to Monroe.

1786.

January	13.	Joseph Jones to Monroe.
February	1.	" "
	9.	
March	14.	..
April	27.	..
June	7.	
	15.	
July	16.	..
	24.	

July	30.	Rufus King to Monroe.
·August	6.	Joseph Jones to Monroe.
	12.	Monroe to Patrick Henry.
	15.	Joseph Jones to Monroe.
	20.	Lambert Cadwalader to Monroe.
October	23.	Joseph Jones to Monroe.
November	22.	William Grayson to Monroe.
December	7.	Joseph Jones to Monroe.

1787.

March	1.	Joseph Jones to Monroe.
	3.	" "
	8.	"
April	30.	William Grayson to Monroe.
May	29.	" "
June	1.	Joseph Jones to Monroe.
	5.	" "
	8.	
	11.	Elbridge Gerry to Monroe.
	18.	Joseph Jones to Monroe.
	22?	" "
July	4.	
August	7.	Edward Carrington to Monroe.
	8.	William Grayson to Monroe.
October	22.	" "

1788.

February	7.	Thomas Jefferson. Extract of letter to Alexander Donald.
May	1 27.	Thomas Jefferson to Edward Carrington.

July   8. Thomas Jefferson to John Brown Cutting.

September 15. Edward Carrington to Monroe.

1790.

January   6. Beverley Randolph to Monroe.

June   25. Elbridge Gerry to Monroe.

             —. James Madison.   Amendments to the Constitution.

1791.

January   15. Richard Henry Lee to Monroe.

             24. Patrick Henry to Monroe.

February   16. George Clinton to Monroe.

             22. Joseph Jones to Monroe.

June   20. ———— to Monroe? [incomplete].

1792.

January   30. George Mason to Monroe.

February   9.   "   "

             20. William Memachan to Monroe.

September   10. Aaron Burr to Monroe.

October   17. Thomas Jefferson to George Washington.

             —. Thomas Jefferson.   Observations on the proposi-
                 tion of a Dutch company to purchase the debt of
                 the United States.

1793.

January   31. George Washington to Madame La Fayette.

May   16. Robert R. Livingston to Monroe.

November   28. Henry Tazewell to Monroe.

1794.

January   4. Robert R. Livingston to Monroe.

             25. Spencer Roane to Monroe.

February   24.   "   "

March	**13.**	Robert R. Livingston to Monroe.
	22.	J. G[arland?] Jefferson to Monroe.
April	**8.**	Robert R. Livingston to Monroe.
	9.	George Washington to Monroe.
	13.	Henry Tazewell to Monroe.
	24.	Thomas Jefferson to Monroe.
May	**30.**	Aaron Burr to Monroe.
June	**1.**	James Monroe to George Washington.
	11.	Alexander Hamilton to Monroe.

August **6.** }
Thermidor **19.** } Thomas Paine to the Convention of France.

16. }
Thermidor **29.** } Thomas Paine to Monroe.

17. }
Thermidor **30.** }   "   [With inclosures].

25. }
Fructidor **8.** }

	28.	John Jay to Monroe.
September	**14.**	Thomas Paine to Monroe.
	14.	Thomas Paine. "Memorial . . . to [Monroe] the Minister . . . of the United States."
	18.	Robert R. Livingston to Monroe.
	25.	Edmund Randolph to Monroe.

October **5.** }
Vendémiaire **14.** } Thomas Paine to Monroe.

	11.	John Swan to Monroe.

13. }
Vendémiaire **22.** } Thomas Paine to Monroe.

21. }
Vendémiaire **30.** }   ..

November   **7.**   Archibald Hamilton Rowan to Monroe.

17.   Edmund Randolph to Monroe.

22.   John Quincy Adams to Monroe.

24.   John Jay to Monroe.

25.   "   "

28.

December   **5.**   James Brown to Monroe.

5.   John Langdon to Monroe.

5.   Edmund Randolph to Monroe.

23.   Rufus King to Monroe.

27.   Monroe to the Committee of Public Safety.

—.   Monroe. Memorandum on his first mission to France.

1795.

January   **11.**   Joseph Fenwick to Monroe.

19.   Pierce Butler to Monroe.

February   **1.**   John Quincy Adams to Monroe.

19.   Robert R. Livingston to Monroe.

23.   John Quincy Adams to Monroe.

March   **6.**   John Adams to Monroe.

23.   John Quincy Adams to Monroe.

30.   "   "

April   **2.**   Monroe to John Adams.

8.   Edmund Randolph to George Hammond.   ,

10.   George Hammond to Edmund Randolph.

13.   Edmund Randolph to George Hammond.

14.   George Hammond to Edmund Randolph.

23.   Robert R. Livingston to Monroe.

April   **24.** Henry Tazewell.   Resolution on the Jay treaty of
1794.

May   **16.** John Quincy Adams to Monroe.

26. Thomas Jefferson to Monroe.

29. Edmund Randolph to Jean Antoine Joseph Fauchet.

June   **5.** George Washington to Monroe.

5. George Washington to Madame La Fayette.   ʻ

24. John Langdon to Monroe.

25. James Monroe to George Logan, Aaron Burr, John
Beckley, Robert R. Livingston, and Thomas
Jefferson.

27. Henry Tazewell to Monroe.

29. Stevens Thomson Mason to Monroe.

30. Pierre Auguste Adet to Edmund Randolph.

July   **5.** Aaron Burr to Monroe.

8. John Quincy Adams to Monroe.

10. Robert R. Livingston to Monroe.

August   **2.** Aaron Burr to Monroe.

6. Melancthon Smith to Monroe.

Thermidor   **15.** } Thomas Paine to Monroe.
28. }

25. Robert R. Livingston to Monroe.

September   **4.** David Humphreys to Monroe.

6. Thomas Jefferson to Monroe.

11. Aaron Burr to Monroe.

18. Benjamin Vaughan to Monroe.

-   **23.**

-   **26.** Robert Montgomery to Monroe.

—. Monroe to James Madison.

October	4.	David Humphreys to Monroe.
	5.	" "
	7.	
	18.	Samuel Bayard to Monroe.
	24.	John Quincy Adams to Monroe.
November	2.	Elbridge Gerry to Monroe.
December	17.	Thomas Boylston Adams to Monroe.
	24.	Aaron Burr to Monroe.
	29.	Thomas Boylston Adams to Monroe.
	—.	Monroe. Exposition of the treaty with Great Britain.
	—.	Rufus King to Monroe.
	—.	Thomas Paine to Monroe.

1796.

January	10.	Monroe to Aaron Burr.
	12.	Monroe to James Madison.
	15.	John Breckinridge to Monroe.
	20.	Monroe to James Madison.
	23.	David Humphreys to Monroe.
February	27.	Monroe to James Madison.
March	2.	Thomas Jefferson to Monroe.
	8.	Monroe to the "Comité de Salut Public de la Convention Nationale de la République Française."
	9.	David Humphreys to Monroe.
	10.	Aaron Burr to Monroe.
	21.	Thomas Jefferson to Monroe.
	24.	Monroe to George Washington.
	31.	John Henry to Monroe.
April	12.	John Langdon to Monroe.

April	14.	George Clinton to Monroe.
	24.	Thomas Jefferson to Philip Mazzei. [Extract.]
	28.	Thomas Boylston Adams to Monroe.
May	5.	Monroe to the Minister of Foreign Affairs, France.
	19.	Henry Tazewell to Monroe.
June	12.	Thomas Jefferson to Monroe.
	20.	John Quincy Adams to Monroe.
July	5.	Monroe to James Madison.
	10.	Thomas Jefferson to Monroe.
	21.	Enoch Edwards to Monroe.
	22.	Timothy Pickering to Monroe.
	—.	Enoch Edwards to Monroe.
August	1.	Rufus King to Monroe.
	11.	" "
September	6.	Aaron Burr to Monroe.
	11.	Enoch Edwards to Monroe.
	19.	Rufus King to Monroe.
October	7.	" "
	19.	
November	18.	
December	3.	Monroe to the Minister of Foreign Affairs, France.
	—.	Monroe to ———. Respecting Algiers.
	—.	Monroe to ———.
	—.	Robert R. Livingston to Monroe.
	—.	Citizens of Philadelphia to Monroe.

1797.

February	8.	Rufus King to Monroe.
March Germinal	28. 8. }	Francesco de Miranda to John B. Prevost.

March	—.	John B. Prevost to Francesco de Miranda.
	—.	John B. Prevost to Monroe.
April	2.	Francesco de Miranda to Monroe.
	4.	Elbridge Gerry to Monroe.
May	30.	Robert Goodloe Harper to William Branch Giles.
	31.	William Branch Giles to Robert Goodloe Harper.
	31.	Robert Goodloe Harper to William Branch Giles.
	—.	" "
June	8.	
	14.	
July	1.	Timothy Pickering to Monroe.
	6.	Monroe to Timothy Pickering.
	8.	" "
	15.	
	17.	Timothy Pickering to Monroe.
	19.	Monroe to Timothy Pickering.
	23.	Robert R. Livingston to Monroe.
	24.	Monroe to Timothy Pickering.
	24.	Timothy Pickering to Monroe.
	24.	" "
	25.	
	31.	Monroe to Timothy Pickering.
	31.	" "
August	15.	Timothy Pickering to Monroe.
September	7.	Thomas Jefferson to Monroe.
	15.	Joseph Fenwick to Monroe.
December	25.	Monroe to Thomas Jefferson.
	—.	Monroe. Amount of compensation as minister to France.

December —. Monroe. Account against the United States while minister to France.

—. Monroe. Paper on his recall.

—. Monroe. "Political project of address on my return from first mission."

—. Monroe. Appeal relating to a controversy with France.

—. Monroe. Essay on probable war with France.

—. Spencer Roane to Monroe.

1798.

February 8. Thomas Jefferson to Monroe.

12. Monroe to Enoch Edwards.

March 8. George Washington to John Nicholas. [Copy by Monroe.]

8. Thomas Jefferson to Monroe.

21. " "

25. John Taylor to Monroe.

April 5. Thomas Jefferson to Monroe.

5. John Dawson to Monroe.

13. Timothy Pickering to John Dawson.

19. Thomas Jefferson to Monroe.

20. Enoch Edwards to Monroe.

21. Enoch Edwards to John Dawson.

Floréal 21. 2. } Henri Grégoire to Monroe.

May 21. Thomas Jefferson to Monroe.

June 1. Monroe to Thomas Jefferson.

10. Enoch Edwards to Monroe.

—. Monroe. Note respecting preceding letter.

July 23. Monroe. Account of payments made to the family of General Lafayette.

October   **17.** John Dawson to Monroe.

        29.   " "   " "

November   **15.** Monroe to Thomas Jefferson.

        16.   " "   " "

        —. Monroe to ——. Respecting Dr. George Logan.

1799.

January   **3.** Thomas Jefferson to Monroe.

        23.   " "   " "

        24. Stevens Thomson Mason to Monroe.

February   **10.** John Dawson to Monroe.

        11. Thomas Jefferson to Monroe.

        19.   "   "

March   **24.** Spencer Roane to Monroe.

        29. John Dawson to Monroe.

July   **10.** William Lee "To all whom it may concerne," respecting house owned by Monroe while in France.

December   **6.** Larkin Smith to Monroe.

        7. Archibald Stuart to Monroe.

       14. Joseph Prentis to Monroe.

       22. St. George Tucker to Monroe.

       23. Monroe to Samuel Prentiss.

       27. John Tyler to Monroe.

       29. St. George Tucker to Monroe.

1800.

January   **—.** Stevens Thomson Mason to Monroe.

February   **16.** Thomas Jefferson to Monroe.

March   **4.** Monroe. Decree containing pension of Mary Dalten. **M.**

March 26. Thomas Jefferson to Monroe.

April 4. Monroe to George William Erving.

13. Thomas Jefferson to Monroe.

29. Stevens Thomson Mason to Monroe.

May 15. " "

20. George William Erving to Monroe.

23. Stevens Thomson Mason to Monroe.

26. Thomas Jefferson to Monroe.

July 12. Monroe to St. George Tucker.

12. Monroe to Thomas McKean.

12. Edmond Charles Genet to Monroe.

14. James Grubb to Monroe.

18. Stevens Thomson Mason to Monroe.

19. St. George Tucker to Monroe.

30. Monroe to Edmond Charles Genet.

August 10. Edmond Charles Genet to Monroe.

September 20. Thomas Jefferson to Monroe.

October 22. Joseph Fenwick to Monroe.

November 6. Hugh Williamson to Monroe.

8. Thomas Jefferson to Monroe.

8. Joseph Fenwick to Monroe.

9. James Madison (Bishop) to Monroe.

22. Joseph Fenwick to Monroe.

December 5. Stevens Thomson Mason to Monroe.

10. Joseph Fenwick to Monroe.

17. George William Erving to Monroe.

20. Thomas Jefferson to Monroe.

22. Stevens Thomson Mason to Monroe.

December   —. Monroe to John Adams.

—. Monroe. "A note founded on the denunciation by Mr. [John] Adams, in his reply to an address from the people of Lancaster."

—. Merlin de Thionville to Monroe.

1801.

January   2. Stevens Thomson Mason to Monroe.

7. St. George Tucker to Monroe.

21. Matthew Clay to Monroe.

23. St. George Tucker to Monroe.

25. George William Erving to Monroe.

February   3. Samuel Jordan Cabell to Monroe.

5. Stevens Thomson Mason to Monroe.

7. Benjamin Hichborn to Monroe.

7. Thomas Mann Randolph to Monroe.

9. George William Erving to Monroe.

9. John Tyler to Monroe.

11.   "   "

11. Matthew Clay to Monroe.

11. John Randolph, jr., to Monroe.

12.   "

12.

12. Littleton Waller Tazewell to Monroe.

13. John Dawson to Monroe.

13. John Hoomes to Monroe.

13. Littleton Waller Tazewell to Monroe.

14. Thomas Mann Randolph to Monroe.

15. Francis Brooke to Monroe.

15. Thomas Jefferson to Monroe.

February   15. Wilson Cary Nicholas to Monroe.

16. John Hoomes to Monroe.

17. Matthew Clay to Monroe.

17. George William Erving to Monroe.

17. Stevens Thomson Mason to Monroe.

17. Everard Meade to Monroe.

17. Wilson Cary Nicholas to Monroe.

17. John Randolph, jr., to Monroe.

18. Monroe to Stevens Thomson Mason and Wilson Cary Nicholas.

19. John Hoomes to Monroe.

20.   "   "

20. John Randolph, jr., to Monroe.

24. Samuel Jordan Cabell to Monroe.

25. St. George Tucker to Monroe.

March   2. Monroe to Thomas Jefferson.

5. Monroe to George William Erving.

12. Monroe to Thomas Jefferson.

14. George William Erving to Monroe.

15. Monroe to Thomas Jefferson.

17. George William Erving to Monroe.

23. Monroe to Thomas Jefferson.

24. Monroe to George William Erving.

24. William Lee to Monroe.

April   9. George William Erving to Monroe.

30. Monroe to Thomas Jefferson.

May   3.

23. William Lee to Monroe.

May   26. Thomas Jefferson to Monroe.

29.   "   "

29.

June   12. Monroe to Robert R. Livingston.

18. James Grubb to Monroe.

20. Thomas Jefferson to Monroe.

July   1. John Taylor to Monroe.

5. Stevens Thomson Mason to Monroe.

12. Monroe to George Clinton.

16. Albert Gallatin to Monroe.

21. Thomas Jefferson to Monroe.

23. William Tudor to Monroe.

November 14. Thomas Jefferson to Monroe.

24.   "   "

December 13.

21. Stevens Thomson Mason to Monroe.

24. John Breckinridge to Monroe

—. Resolution offered to Virginia General Assembly.

1802.

January   27. Stevens Thomson Mason to Monroe.

March   17. James Madison (Bishop) to Monroe.

May   3. Monroe.   State grants of land to Jonathan Dainty. **M.**

9. John Shore to Monroe.

June   22. Daniel Clark to James Madison.   [With inclosures.]

22. Richard Parker to Monroe.

August   4. Meriwether Jones to Monroe.

October   18. Monroe.   Grant of land in Berkley County to James Welch, assignee of John Dixon.   **M.**

November 3. Edward Livingston. Answer to question proposed by Jared Ingersoll, William Rawle, Joseph Borden McKean, and Peter Stephen Du Ponceau.

27. James Madison to Charles Pinckney.

December 6. James Pendleton to Monroe.

1803.

January 3. John Randolph, jr., to Monroe.

7. Monroe to Thomas Jefferson.

10. Thomas Jefferson to Monroe.

13.   "   "

18. Robert R. Livingston to Talleyrand-Perigord.

29. Edmond Charles Genet to Monroe.

February 23. United States, Senate. Resolutions respecting the navigation of the Mississippi River.

26. Stevens Thomson Mason to Monroe.

26. United States, Senate. A bill directing a detachment from the militia of the United States, and for erecting certain arsenals.

26. United States. An act, etc., making further provision for the expenses attending the intercourse between the United States and foreign nations.

March 1. Wilson Cary Nicholas to Monroe.

2. James Madison to Robert R. Livingston and Monroe.

4. John Pintard to Monroe.

Ventôse 9. }
              19. } Talleyrand-Perigord to Robert R. Livingston.

16. Robert R. Livingston to Talleyrand-Perigord.

Germinal 21. }
                1. } Talleyrand-Perigord to Robert R. Livingston.

—. John Pintard. Notes on the Mississippi River, East and West Florida.

March   —.   Thomas Lopez. Prospectus of "Atlas Geografico de la America."

April   9.   Monroe to James Madison. **L. B.**

       10.   Robert R. Livingston to Monroe.

       12.   Monroe to Robert R. Livingston.

       12.   Robert R. Livingston to Monroe.

       13.   Monroe to Robert R. Livingston.

Germinal   **13.**   ⎫ Talleyrand-Perigord to Robert R. Livingston.
            23.   ⎭

       13.   Robert R. Livingston to Monroe.

       13.   Robert R. Livingston to Talleyrand-Perigord.

       15.   Monroe to James Madison. **L. B.**

       15.   Monroe to James Madison. "Not sent."

       17.   Robert R. Livingston to Monroe.

       19.   Monroe to James Madison. **L. B.**

       19.   Robert R. Livingston to Monroe.

       23?   Barbé Marbois. Project of a treaty between United States and France.

       30.   Monroe. Articles of agreement to a treaty with France for the cession of Louisiana.

       30.   Monroe to Talleyrand-Perigord.

       —.   Robert R. Livingston and Monroe. Project of a treaty between United States and France.

May   2.   Monroe. Journal of cession of Louisiana.

       3.   Robert R. Livingston to Monroe.

Floréal   **3.**   ⎫ Barbé Marbois to Robert R. Livingston and Monroe.
            14. ⎭

       5.   Monroe to Robert R. Livingston.

       6.   "   "

       9.   Monroe and Robert R. Livingston to Rufus King. **L. B.**

May
Floréal
  9.
20. } Barbé Marbois to Monroe and Robert R. Livingston.

Floréal
  12.
23. } Barbé Marbois to Monroe.

13. Robert R. Livingston to Monroe.

13. Monroe and Robert R. Livingston to James Madison. **L. B.**

16. Monroe to Charles Pinckney. **L. B.**

18. Monroe to James Madison. **L. B.**

19. Monroe and Robert R. Livingston to Barbé Marbois. **L. B.**

19. Monroe to Talleyrand-Perigord. **L. B.**

Floréal
  19.
30. } Barbé Marbois to Monroe.

23. Monroe to James Madison. **L. B.**

23. George William Erving to Monroe.

25. Monroe to Stevens Thomson Mason, Wilson Cary Nicholas, and John Breckenridge.

28. Robert R. Livingston to Monroe.

28. Robert R. Livingston to Charles Pinckney.

31. Robert R. Livingston to Monroe.

31. James Madison to Monroe.

June
2. Monroe and Robert R. Livingston to Barbé Marbois.

2. Robert R. Livingston to Barbé Marbois.

2.   " "   " "

3.

7. Monroe to James Madison. **L. B.**

7. Monroe. Opinion respecting West Florida. **L. B.**

7. Monroe and Robert R. Livingston to James Madison. **L. B.**

Prairial
  7.
19? } Talleyrand-Perigord to Monroe.

June

7. Monroe and Robert R. Livingston to Charles Pinckney. **L. B.**

8. Monroe to James Madison. **L. B.**

9. Monroe to Talleyrand-Perigord.

15. Monroe to Robert R. Livingston.

15. John Randolph, jr., to Monroe.

19. Monroe to James Madison. **L. B.**

20. John Graham to Monroe.

Messidor

20. ⎫
2. ⎬ Barbé Marbois to Monroe.

Messidor

21. ⎫
3. ⎬ Talleyrand-Perigord to Monroe.

23. John Mercer. "Extracts from my journal, commencing . . . the day on wh. I sailed from New York for France."

23. Monroe to Robert R. Livingston.

23. Monroe to James Madison.

23. James Yard to Monroe.

25. James Madison to Monroe.

28. Monroe to Robert R. Livingston.

29. Monroe to Talleyrand-Perigord.

July

5. Monroe to Charles Pinckney. **L. B.**

12. Monroe to d'Azara. **L. B.**

14. D'Azara to Monroe. **L. B.**

17. Robert R. Livingston to Monroe.

19. Monroe to James Madison. **L. B.**

20.　　"　　　　　"　　**L. B.**

26.　　··　　　　··　　**L. B.**

26. William Bingham to Monroe.

Thermidor

29. ⎫
11. ⎬ Barbé Marbois to Monroe.

July   30. James Madison to Monroe.

—. Robert R. Livingston to Monroe.

—. Rufus King to James Madison.

—. Thomas Paine.   Notes on Louisiana.

August   11. Monroe to James Madison.   **L. B.**

12. Delamotte to Monroe.

15. Monroe to James Madison.   **L. B.**

19. Barbé Marbois to Monroe.

20. Monroe to Robert R. Livingston.

20. Monroe to Barbé Marbois.

20. Barbé Marbois to Monroe.

31. Monroe to James Madison.   **L. B.**

September 9. Robert R. Livingston to Monroe.

11.   "   "

Fructidor 11. 25. } Barbé Marbois to Monroe.

25. Robert R. Livingston to Monroe.

29. Monroe to James Madison.   **L. B.**

—. Robert R. Livingston to Monroe.

—.   "   "

—.

—.

—.

—.

—.

—.

—. Monroe to James Madison.

—. Thomas Sumter to Monroe.

October   **1.**   Thomas Sumter.   Memorandum relative to Florida, etc.

Vendémiaire 12. $\left.\begin{array}{l} \textbf{3.} \\ \end{array}\right\}$ Barbé Marbois to Monroe.

        8.   Robert R. Livingston to Monroe.

        9.   Monroe to Robert R. Livingston.

    10.   Monroe to Barbé Marbois.

    17.   Sir Francis Baring to Monroe.

    19.   Monroe to Robert R. Livingston.

    21.   Monroe to James Madison.   **L. B.**

    22.   Monroe to James Madison.

    28.   Robert R. Livingston to Monroe.

    29.   Monroe to Robert R. Livingston.

November **2.** $\left.\begin{array}{l} \\ \end{array}\right\}$ Barbé Marbois to Monroe. [With inclosures.]
Brumaire 12.

     6.   John Mercer to Monroe.

     7.   John Randolph, jr., to Monroe.

    12.   John Taylor to Monroe.

    14.   Baring Brothers to Marbois.

    14.   Charles Pinckney to Monroe.

    15.   Nathaniel Macon to Monroe.

    16.   Monroe to James Madison.   **L. B.**

    19.   Monroe to Robert R. Livingston

    25.   Monroe to James Madison.

    25.   Robert R. Livingston to Monroe.   **L. B.**

    29.   Monroe to the Governor of Virginia.

    29.   Monroe to Lord Hawkesbury.   **L. B.**

December   **10.**   Robert R. Livingston to Monroe.

    15.   Monroe to James Madison.

December   17.   Monroe to James Madison.

         23.   James Madison (Bishop) to Monroe.

         26.   James Madison to Monroe.

         •—.   Monroe to John Taylor.

         —.   Monroe to Robert R. Livingston.   " Not sent."

         —.

         —.   Monroe.   Notes on negotiations with France rela-
tive to cession of Louisiana.

         —.   Monroe.   Political reflections on the acquisition of
Louisiana.

         —.   Anonymous to Monroe.

         —.   Anonymous.   "An Examination into the Boundar-
ies of Louisiana."

         —.   Anonymous.   " Opinion respecting West Florida."

         —.   Anonymous.   "Chronological series of facts rela-
tive to Louisiana."

         —.   Anonymous.   "A list of instructions and other
papers relating to the negotiations for the acqui-
sition of Louisiana."

         —.   Cipher of Robert R. Livingston.

1804.

January   4.   William Pinkney to Monroe.

         5.   James Madison to Monroe.   [With inclosure.]

         8.   Thomas Jefferson to Monroe.

         9.   Monroe to James Madison.   **L. B.**

        13.   Monroe to Robert R. Livingston.

        13.   Monroe to ———— Disbrowe [?].

        19.   James Madison to Monroe.

        22.   Monroe to Wilson Cary Nicholas.

        23.   Monroe to Christopher Gore.

January	**27.**	Monroe to the American Commissioners.
February	**2.**	Charles Pinckney to Monroe.
	8.	Monroe to Sir Francis Baring.
	10.	Pedro Cevallos to Charles Pinckney.
	14.	Monroe to Robert R. Livingston.
	14.	Monroe to Barbé Marbois.
	14.	James Madison to Monroe. [With inclosures.]
	22.	Charles Pinckney to Monroe.
	23.	Christopher Gore and William Pinkney to Monroe.
	23.	Commissioners [J. Trumbull, M. Swabey, J. Anstey, Christopher Gore, and William Pinkney] to James Madison.
	23.	Minutes of meeting of the Commissioners under the treaty.
	25.	Monroe to James Madison. **L. B.**
	26.	" "
	28.	John Randolph to Monroe.
March	**3.**	Monroe to James Madison.
	3.	Monroe to Christopher Gore and William Pinkney.
	8.	Robert R. Livingston to Monroe.
	14.	John Page to Monroe.
	15.	Monroe to Thomas Jefferson.
	15.	Robert R. Livingston to Monroe.
	17.	Casa Yrujo to James Madison.
	18.	Monroe to James Madison. **L. B.**
	19.	Monroe to ———.
	19.	James Madison to Casa Yrujo.
Ventôse	**20.** **30.**	} Barbé Marbois to Monroe.
	27.	Monroe to Count de Woronzow. **L. B.**

March   —.   Robert R. Livingston to Monroe.

April   4.   Monroe to Lord Hawkesbury.   **L. B.**

7.   "   "   **L. B.**

7.   Monroe to G—— Taylor.   •

7.   Monroe.   Project of convention relative to seamen, etc., transmitted to Lord Hawkesbury.

9.   Robert R. Livingston to Monroe.

13.   Monroe to Charles Pinckney.

15.   Monroe to James Madison.   **L. B.**

16.   Monroe to Robert R. Livingston.

17.   Monroe to James Madison.

26.   "   "

Floréal   27.
8.   } Barbé Marbois to Hope & Co.

May   1.   Monroe to Lord Hawkesbury.   **L. B.**

1.   Horr Brown Trist to Monroe.

1.   Vincente Folcbe to William C. C. Claiborne.

3.   Monroe to James Madison.   **L. B.**

5.   "   "

6.

11.   John Mercer to Monroe.

13.   Monroe to Robert R. Livingston.

16.   Monroe to Lord Hawkesbury.   **L. B.**

16.   Monroe to Lord Harrowby.   **L. B.**

16.   Robert R. Livingston to Monroe.

16.   Sir William Scott to Monroe.   **L. B.**

18.   Monroe to William Pinkney.   **L. B.**

18.   Monroe to Sir William Scott.   **L. B.**

22.   Monroe to James Madison.

May   **22.** Robeit R. Livingston to Monioe.

23. Monioe to William Pinkney.

24. Monroe to Lord Haiiowby.   **L. B.**

25. James Madison to Monroe.

30. Robert R. Livingston to Monioe.

30. William C. C. Claiborne to James Madison.

31. Monioe to Robert R. Livingston.

June   **1.** Monioe to Sii S——— Cottiell.   **L. B.**

2. William C. C. Claiboine to James Madison.

2. William C. C. Claiboine to Governor Folche.

3. Monioe to James Madison.   **L. B.**

5. Monioe to Lord Hawkesbury.   **L. B.**

5. Monioe to ——— Biooke.   **L. B.**

8. Monioe to John Meicei.

10. Monioe to James Madison.

12.   "   "

17. John Meicei to Monioe.

18. Monioe to James Madison.   **L. B.**

18. Monioe to J—— Mackenzie and A—— Glennie.
       L. B.

19. Monioe to John Meicer.

19. Robeit R. Livingston to Monroe.

20. Monioe to J—— J—– Murray.   **L. B.**

21. Monioe to Robeit R. Livingston.

22. Monroe to Loid Haiiowby.   **L. B.**

23. Monioe to James Madison.   **L. B.**

25. Monioe to consuls of the United States.   **L. B.**

28. Monioe to James Madison.

—. John Lowell to Monioe.

July   **1.** Monroe to James Madison.

15. Robert R. Livingston to Monroe.

15–21. Anonymous.   Diary.

20. John Randolph to Monroe.

21. James Madison to Monroe.

August   **4.** Monroe to Robert R. Livingston.

5. Monroe to John Mercer.

7. Monroe to James Madison.   **L. B.**

9. Lord Harrowby to Monroe.   **L. B.**

10. Monroe to James Madison.

11. Monroe to Lord Harrowby.   **L. B.**

11. Monroe to United States consuls in England.   **L. B.**

16. J——- Barlow to George Hammond.   **L. B.**

21. Monroe to Lord Harrowby.   **L. B.**

22. Lord Harrowby to Monroe.   **L. B**

23. John Mercer to Monroe.

23. Robert R. Livingston to Monroe.

24. Monroe to Robert R. Livingston.

25. Lord Harrowby to Monroe.   **L. B.**

28. Monroe to Lord Harrowby.   **L. B.**

30. William Pinkney to Monroe.

September   **3.** Lord Harrowby to Monroe.   **L. B.**

5. Monroe to Lord Harrowby.   **L. B.**

5. Monroe.   Note respecting the boundary of United States.   **L. B.**

8. Monroe to James Madison.   **L. B**

12. James Madison to Monroe.

14. Monroe to James Madison.

September **15.** Robert R. Livingston to Monroe.

15. Lord Harrowby to Monroe. **L. B.**

17. Monroe to James Madison. **L. B.**

21. Monroe to George Hammond. **L. B.**

23. George William Erving to Monroe.

25. Monroe to Thomas Jefferson.

26. Monroe to Lord Harrowby. **L. B.**

26. Lord Harrowby to Monroe. **L. B.**

27. W—— Fawkener to George Hammond. **L. B.**

28. Lord Harrowby to Monroe. **L. B.**

29. Monroe to Lord Harrowby. **L. B.**

29.   ‟

29. Lord Harrowby to Monroe. **L. B.**

29.   ‟   ‟

October **3.** Monroe to James Madison.

3. Monroe to George Hammond. **L. B.**

3. St. George Tucker to Monroe.

5. Monroe to United States consuls in England. **L. B.**

5. J—— d'Anduagas to Monroe.

15. James Madison to Casa Yrujo.

18. George William Erving to Monroe.

21. Casa Yrujo to James Madison.

25. James Madison to Casa Yrujo.

26. James Madison to Charles Pinckney.

26. James Madison to Monroe.

26.   ‟   ‟

—. Casa Yrujo to Madison.

November **6.** Monroe to Robert R. Livingston.

8. Monroe to Talleyrand-Perigord.

November   **12.**   Robert R. Livingston to Monroe.

          12.   Charles Pinckney to Monroe.

          13.   Monroe to Robert R. Livingston.

          18.   Charles Pinckney to Monroe.

          19.   Robert R. Livingston to Monroe.

          23.   Monroe to Barbé Marbois.

          25.   John Armstrong to Monroe.

Frimaire   **28.** } Barbé Marbois to Monroe.
          8. }

          —.   Barbé Marbois to Monroe ?

December   **10.**   George William Erving to Monroe.

          16.   Monroe to James Madison.

Frimaire   **20.** } Talleyrand-Perigord to Monroe.
          30. }

          24.   John Armstrong to Monroe.

          —.   Notes relative to a letter from William Branch Giles on the conduct of Monroe in the negotiations for cession of Louisiana.

          —.   L—— Callaghan.   Address to the Minister of Marine of France.

1805.

January   **11.**   Albert Gallatin to James Madison.   **L. B.**

          19.   De P ——— to H ———.

April   **16.**   George William Erving to Monroe.

June   **12.**   James Bowdoin to Monroe.

          15.   Thomas Jefferson to Monroe.

July   **31.**   Monroe to Lord Mulgrave.   **L. B.**

August   **5.**   Lord Mulgrave to Monroe.   **L. B.**

          6.   Monroe to James Madison.   **L. B.**

          8.   Monroe to Lord Mulgrave.   **L. B.**

August	9.	Lord Mulgrave to Monroe.	**L. B.**
	10.	W—— Lyman to Monroe.	**L. B.**
	12.	Lord Mulgrave to Monroe.	**L. B.**
	12.	Monroe to Lord Mulgrave.	**L. B.**
	12.	" "	**L. B.**
	16.	Monroe to James Madison.	**L. B.**
	16.	Monroe to Lord Mulgrave.	**L. B.**
	17.	Lord Mulgrave to Monroe.	**L. B.**
	20.	Monroe to James Madison.	**L. B.**
	20.	Monroe to James Madison.	**L. B.**
	27.	John Murray Forbes to Monroe.	
September	23.	Monroe to Lord Mulgrave.	**L. B.**
	25.	Monroe to James Madison.	**L. B.**
October	9.	Lord Mulgrave to Monroe.	**L. B.**
	10.	Monroe to Lord Mulgrave.	**L. B.**
	11.	" "	**L. B.**
	12.	Lord Mulgrave to Monroe.	**L. B.**
	13.	Monroe. Memorandum of papers given to James Bowdoin.	
	18.	Monroe to James Madison.	**L. B.**
	27.	Lord Mulgrave to Monroe.	**L. B.**
	28.	Monroe to Lord Mulgrave.	**L. B.**
	28.	Monroe to W—— Lyman.	**L. B.**
November	11.	Monroe to James Madison.	**L. B.**
	13.	Monroe to James Bowdoin.	**L. B.**
	14.	Monroe to John Armstrong.	**L. B.**
	24.	J. Cox Barnet to Monroe.	
	25.	Lord Mulgrave to Monroe.	**L. B.**

November 26. Monroe to James Madison.   **L. B.**

26. Monroe to Lord Mulgrave.   **L. B.**

29.   "   **L. B.**

December 11. Monroe to James Madison.   **L. B.**

16.   "   ✓   "   **L. B.**

23.   **L. B.**

—.

—. Monroe to King of Spain.

1806.

January   6. James Sullivan to Monroe.

7. John Armstrong to Monroe.

10. Monroe to James Madison.

11. Monroe to Thomas Jefferson.

•   13. A—— Barnitz to Monroe.

20. James Bowdoin to Monroe.

28. Monroe to James Madison.   **L. B.**

February   2.   "   "

5. George William Erving to Monroe.

5. James Bowdoin to Monroe.

7. Charles James Fox to Monroe.   **L. B.**

8. Monroe to Charles James Fox.   **L. B.**

12. Monroe to James Madison.   **L. B.**

23. Charles James Fox to Monroe.   **L. B.**

25. Monroe to Charles James Fox.   **L. B.**

25.   "   "   **L. B.**

27. John Armstrong to Monroe.

27. John Taylor to Monroe.

28. Monroe to James Madison.

March   **4.** Monroe to Baring Brothers & Co.

        11. Monroe to James Madison. **L. B.**

        11. Monroe to John Armstrong. **L. B.**

        11. Monroe to James Bowdoin. **L. B.**

        14. Monroe to Baring Brothers & Co. **L. B.**

        14. Baring Brothers & Co. to Monroe.

        16. Thomas Jefferson to Monroe.

        18. Monroe to Baring Brothers & Co.

        18. Thomas Jefferson to Monroe.

        20. John Randolph to Monroe.

        31. Monroe to James Madison. **L. B.**

        31. Monroe to Charles James Fox. **L. B.**

April   **3.** Monroe to James Madison. **.L. B.**

        8. Charles James Fox to Monroe.

        9. Monroe to United States consuls in England. **L. B.**

       10. Monroe to Charles James Fox. **L. B.**

       16. Lord Morton to Monroe. **L. B.**

       16? Sir F——- Vincent to Monroe. **L. B.**

       17. Charles James Fox to Monroe. **L. B.**

       18. Monroe to Secretary of State, James Madison. **L. B.**

       20.   "   "   **L. B.**

       22. John Randolph to Monroe.

       25. Thomas Mullett to Monroe.

       26. Monroe to Charles James Fox. **L. B.**

       28. Monroe to James Madison. **L. B.**

       29.   "   "

       30. Monroe to Sir S—— Cottrell. **L. B.**

May   **2.** Monroe to United States consuls in England. **L. B.**

May

2. Monroe to Charles James Fox. **L. B.**

4. Thomas Jefferson to Monroe.

9. James Sullivan to Monroe.

13. Monroe to C—— Murray. **L. B.**

13. J. Cox Barnet to Monroe.

13. George Sullivan to Monroe.

14. James Madison (Bishop) to Monroe.

16. Charles James Fox to Monroe. **L. B.**

17. Monroe to James Madison. **L. B.**

17. James Madison to Monroe.

17. Monroe to United States consuls in England. **L. B.**

19. Monroe to Charles James Fox. **L. B.**

20. Monroe to James Madison. **L. B.**

20. Charles James Fox to Monroe. **L. B.**

21. Monroe to Charles James Fox. **L. B.**

23. George William Erving to Monroe.

28. Monroe. Notes respecting Spain and Great Britain.

28. Col. Richard O'Brien to H—— D——

30. John Armstrong to Monroe.

June

5. Charles James Fox to Monroe. **L. B.**

9. Monroe to James Madison. **L. B.**

10. William Wirt to Monroe.

15. Monroe to Thomas Jefferson. "Not sent."

16. Monroe to John Randolph.

18. George William Erving to Monroe.

19. William Pinkney to Monroe.

20. Monroe to James Bowdoin.

20. Monroe to Thomas Jefferson.

June

21. Monroe to John Armstrong.

21. Monroe to Charles James Fox. **L. B.**

22. Charles James Fox to Monroe. **L. B.**

22. W—— Marsden to Vice-Admiral Berkeley. **L. B.**

23. Monroe to Charles James Fox. **L. B.**

23. Monroe to William Pinkney.

25. Monroe to Charles James Fox. **L. B.**

27. Monroe to Sir F—— Vincent. **L. B.**

27. Sir F—— Vincent to Monroe.

July

1. Monroe to William Pinkney.

1. William Pinkney to Monroe.

2.   ''   ''

3. John Randolph to Monroe.

4. J—— M—— Taylor to Monroe.

4. William Pinkney to Monroe.

5. Monroe to De Witt Clinton.

5. Monroe to William Pinkney.

8? Monroe to Thomas Jefferson.

9. John Armstrong to Monroe.

17. Monroe to William Pinkney.

23. William Pinkney to Monroe.

24. John Murray Forbes to Monroe.

25. Monroe to William Pinkney.

25. William Pinkney to Monroe.

26. Charles James Fox to Monroe. **L. B.**

31. Monroe to Charles James Fox. **L. B.**

—. Monroe. "Rough sketch of a joint letter for Mr. [William] Pinkney and myself."

August   2. William Pinkney to Monroe.

2. J—— M—— Taylor to Monroe.

4. Monroe to Charles James Fox.   **L. B.**

11. George William Erving to Monroe.

29. Monroe to James Sullivan.

30. Monroe to Doctor —— Eustace.

—. William Pinkney to Monroe.

—.   ''   ''

September   6. W—— Marsden to Sir F—— Vincent.   **L. B.**

8. Charles James Fox to Monroe.   **L. B.**

13. Monroe to James Madison.   **L. B.**

15. Lord Spencer to Monroe.   **L. B.**

16. Monroe to Lord Spencer.   **L. B.**

16. John Randolph to Monroe.

18.   ''   ''   [Extract by Monroe.]

24. Lord Spencer to Monroe.   **L. B.**

24. Lord Howick to Monroe.   **L. B.**

24. J—— Stewart to Forsyth, Smith & Co.

25. Monroe to Lord Spencer.   **L. B.**

25. Monroe to Lord Howick.   **L. B.**

25. Lord Howick to Monroe.   **L. B.**

29.   ''   ''   **L. B.**

—. William Pinkney to Monroe.

October   2. Lord Howick to Monroe.   **L. B.**

4. Extract of order for court-martial of Capt. H——
   Whitby for the murder of John Price.   **L. B.**

6. Monroe to Lord Howick.   **L. B.**

11. Lord Howick to Monroe.   **L. B.**

October   **16.** C—— Bicknell to Monroe. **L. B.**

16. Monroe to C—— Bicknell. **L. B.**

18. Thomas Grenville to Lord Howiek. **L. B.**

20. Monroe to Lord Howiek. **L. B.**

22. Lord Howick to Monroe. **L. B.**

23. Lords Commissioners of the Admiralty to Lord Howiek. **L. B.**

24. Monroe to James Madison. **L. B.**

25. Lord Howiek to Monroe. **L. B.**

26. Thomas Jefferson to Monroe.

27. Monroe to James Madison. **L. B.**

—. J—— Dorr to Monroe.

November   **1.** William Pinkney to Monroe.

4.   "   "

4.

4. Lord Auckland to Monroe.

9. Monroe to William Pinkney.

9. William Pinkney to Monroe.

14. Monroe to William Pinkney.

14. Monroe to Lord Holland.

17. William Pinkney to Monroe.

December   **5.**   "   "

5. John Randolph to Monroe.

10. Monroe to William Pinkney.

11. —— Williams to Monroe.

11. William Pinkney to Monroe.

31. Monroe to Baring Brothers & Co.

31. Monroe and William Pinkney to Lords Holland and Auckland.

December **31.** Monroe and William Pinkney. Copy of treaty of amity, commerce, and navigation between His Britannic Majesty and the United States of America.

31. Lords Holland and Auckland to Monroe and William Pinkney.

—. William Pinkney to Monroe.

—.   "   "

—.

—.

—.

—.

—.

—.

—.

—. Project for a treaty of amity, commerce, and navigation between Great Britain and United States.

—. Monroe. Memorandum relating to the balance of trade between United States and Great Britain.

—. Observations on 1st and 2d paragraphs of the treaty between Great Britain and United States.

—. Copy of the proposed alterations of treaty between Great Britain and United States.

—. Monroe. "A project wh. I prepared—of a treaty."

—. Monroe. Note regarding the proposed treaty.

—. Monroe. Memorandum regarding the proposed treaty.

—. Monroe. Draft for articles of the proposed treaty.

—. Monroe. Draft for articles of the proposed treaty on the "Intercourse between the U. States and European dominions."

—. Monroe. Amendments to articles 6, 9, 12, 23, and 24 of the proposed treaty.

December —. Monroe. Draft of article relating to desertions in the proposed treaty.

—. Monroe. Notes of a letter to ———.

—. James Bowdoin and Monroe. "Loose thots respecting ye commercial part of a Treaty between Great Britain & ye United States."

—. William Tudor, jr. Statement regarding the commerce between Nova Scotia and the United States.

—. Anonymous. Extracts respecting conduct of Yrujo.

—. Draft of article relating to trade, tonnage, duties, etc.

1807.

January —. Lord Auckland to Monroe.

2. John Randolph to Monroe. [With a postscript.]

3. Monroe and William Pinkney to James Madison.

3. Littleton Waller Tazewell to Monroe.

—. William Pinkney to Monroe.

—.   " '   "

—.

—.

—.

—.

—.

7. Lord Auckland to Monroe.

7.   " '

9. G—— W—— Hammond to Monroe.

10. Monroe to James Madison.

12.   "   "

13. Lord Holland to Monroe.

16. Monroe and William Pinkney to John Armstrong.

January   20. William Pinkney to Monroe.

24. Geoige William Eiving to Monroe.

27. William Pinkney to Monroe.

February   1. J—— Allen to Monroe.

3. James Madison to Monroe and William Pinkney.

4. Loid Auckland to Monroe.

10. Loids Holland and Auckland to Monroe and William Pinkney.

11. Monroe to William Pinkney.

16. William Pinkney to Monroe.

18.   "   "

22. Loid Auckland to Monroe.

23. William Pinkney to Monroe.

24. Loid Auckland to Monroe.

25. Monroe to William Pinkney.

27. James Bowdoin to Monroe.

—. Loid Holland to Monroe.

March   2. Loid Auckland to Monroe.

4. William Bianch Giles to Monroe.

5. Loid Howick to Monroe.

6. Monroe to Loid Howick.

11. William Pinkney to Monroe.

11. Loid Howick to Monroe.

13. Eail of Selkiik to Loid Holland.

16. William Pinkney to Monroe.

18. James Madison to Monroe.

21. Thomas Jeffeison to Monroe.

23. Loid Auckland to Monroe.

March   **24.** John Randolph to Monroe.

24. Lord Holland to Monroe.

24. Lord Auckland to Monroe.

26. Lord Holland to Monroe.

27. Lord Auckland to Monroe.

28. Lord Holland to Monroe.

31. Monroe and William Pinkney to Lord Holland.

31. William Pinkney to Monroe.

—.   "   "

—.

—. Lord Holland to Monroe.

—.   "   "

April   **2.** Monroe to George Canning.

4. John Armstrong to Monroe and William Pinkney.

4. James Bowdoin to John Armstrong.

5. James Bowdoin to Monroe.

6. William Pinkney to Monroe.

6. John Armstrong to James Bowdoin.

9. Pennsylvania legislature. Proceedings relative to the Cumberland road.

11. Monroe to George Canning.

12. Joseph Hopper Nicholson to Monroe.

13. Monroe to George Canning.

15. George Canning to Monroe and William Pinkney.

16. William Pinkney to Monroe.

17. John Randolph to Monroe.

22. Monroe and William Pinkney to James Madison.

24. William Pinkney to Monroe.

April	**25.**	Monroe and William Pinkney to James Madison.
	29.	Monroe to George Canning.
	30.	Monroe to William Branch Giles.
May	**4.**	Monroe to Littleton Waller Tazewell.
	6.	Monroe to William Pinkney.
	7.	Monroe and William Pinkney to James Madison.
	9.	William Pinkney to Monroe.
	11.	''
	18.	Lord Holland to Monroe.
	20.	James Madison to Monroe.
	29.	Thomas Jefferson to Monroe.
	30.	John Randolph to Monroe.
	—.	Littleton Waller Tazewell to Monroe.
June	**16.**	William Pinkney to Monroe.
	20.	Richard O'Brien to ———.
	27.	Lord Holland to Monroe.
	30.	John Mullowny to Thomas Jefferson.
	—.	Monroe to Thomas Jefferson.
July	**6.**	James Madison to Monroe.
	6.	Nicholas Biddle to Monroe.
	7.	John Armstrong to Monroe.
	15.	James Bowdoin to Monroe.
	18.	Monroe and William Pinkney to George Canning.
	18.	George Canning to Monroe and William Pinkney.
	23.	Monroe and William Pinkney to James Madison.
	24.	Monroe and William Pinkney to George Canning.
	25.	George Canning to Monroe.
	27.	Monroe to George Canning.

July   **28.** Lords Holland and Auckland to George Canning.

              29. Monroe to George Canning.

              30. Monroe and William Pinkney to George Canning.

August   **3.** George Canning to Monroe.

              4. Monroe to James Madison.

              6. Monroe to George Canning.

              8. George Canning to Monroe.

              9. Monroe to George Canning.

              14. Monroe to James Madison.

September   **1.** Monroe to George Canning.

              7.   ''   ''

              9.

              16. Monroe to James Madison.

              22. Lord Auckland to Monroe.

              23. George Canning to Monroe.

              25. Monroe to Lord Auckland.

              29. Monroe to George Canning.

October   **2.** William Pinkney to Monroe.

              6. Monroe to William Pinkney.

              6. Monroe to George Canning.

              6. S—— Cottrell to Monroe.

              9. Monroe to George Canning.

              9. George Canning to James Madison.

              10. Monroe and William Pinkney to James Madison.

              10. Monroe to John Armstrong.

              14. Lord Holland to Monroe.

              15. Lord Erskine to Monroe.

              17. George Rose to Monroe.

October   **18.** Monroe and William Pinkney to George Canning.

20. George Rose to Monroe.

20.   "   "

21. Lord Erskine to Monroe.

22. Monroe and William Pinkney to James Madison.

22. George Rose to Monroe.

22. George Canning to Monroe and William Pinkney.

22. George Canning to Monroe.

23. Monroe to George Rose.

23. Monroe to George Canning.

23. George Canning to Monroe.

25. Edward Disbrowe to Monroe.

28. Monroe to James Madison.

28. Monroe to the Governor of Maryland.

29. Monroe to George Canning.

31. Nicholas Biddle to Monroe.

—. Monroe to James Madison.

—. Lord Holland to Monroe.

November   **1.** Monroe to Lord Holland.

2. William Pinkney to Monroe.

6. Monroe to William Pinkney.

6. Lord Auckland to Monroe.

26. Charles Blagden to Monroe.

—. Monroe to Alexander Baring.

—. Monroe to William Pinkney.

December   **10.** Richard O'Brien to ——.

24. John Randolph to Monroe.

25. John Clopton to Alexander McCrae.

December   **30.** Thomas Paine to Monroe.

—. Robert Liston. Proposed addition to the treaty with Great Britain of 1794.

—. Notes relative to a memorial of Canadian merchants to Lords Holland and Auckland.

—. Arthur J. Stansbury to Monroe.

—. United States, House of Representatives. Report of Committee of Commerce and Manufactures.

1808.

January   **2.** Nicholas Biddle to Monroe.

2. William W. Morris to Monroe.

18. Walter Jones to Monroe.

20.   " "   " "

24. Monroe to Walter Jones.

February   **3.** Monroe to James Madison.

8. William Wirt to Monroe.

18. Thomas Jefferson to Monroe.

22. John Taylor to Monroe.

27. Monroe to Thomas Jefferson.

29. M—— Clay to Monroe.

March   **5.** Monroe to James Madison.

9. John Randolph to Monroe.

10. John Minor to Monroe.

10. Thomas Jefferson to Monroe.

20. John Taylor to Monroe.

22. Monroe to Thomas Jefferson.

23. Monroe to John Randolph.

26. Monroe to James Madison.

26. John Randolph to Monroe.

March	28.	Monroe to James Madison.
April	4.	Timothy Pickering to Monroe.
	5.	Monroe to James Madison.
	6.	Monroe to ———.
	6.	"
	8.	George William Erving to Monroe
	11.	Thomas Jefferson to Monroe.
	13.	" "
	18.	Monroe to Timothy Pickering.
	18.	Monroe to Thomas Jefferson.
June	23.	James Bowdoin to Monroe.
September	13.	Monroe to Thomas Jefferson.
	27.	" "
	28.	Thomas Jefferson to Monroe.
October	8.	Littleton Waller Tazewell to Monroe.
	12.	Thomas Jefferson to Monroe.
	13.	" "
	15.	Eliza Bonaparte to Monroe.
	24.	Monroe to Thomas Jefferson.
	28.	" "
	30.	Monroe to Littleton Waller Tazewell.
November	1.	Monroe to Thomas Jefferson.
	6.	Monroe to Eliza Bonaparte.
	7.	James Bowdoin to Monroe.
	18.	Nicholas Biddle to Monroe.
December	20.	Monroe to William Wirt.
	26.	J—- L—— Taylor to Monroe.
	20.	William Wirt to Monroe.

December —. Monroe. "Notes not used" of letter to Thomas Jefferson.

  —. Monroe to Charles Johnson

  —. Monroe to John Randolph.   ,

  —. Monroe to ——.

  —.   " "

1809.

January 1. John Randolph to Monroe.

  7.   " "   " "

  9. Monroe to Nicholas Biddle.

  9. Monroe to John Taylor.

  15. John Taylor to Monroe.

  18. Monroe to Thomas Jefferson.

  28. Thomas Jefferson to Monroe.

February 7. Monroe to David Gelston.

  15. John Mullowny to Thomas Jefferson.

March 2. Thomas Jefferson to John Mullowny.

May 25. John Mercer to Monroe.

September 4. Monroe to Thomas Jefferson.

October 19. Edward Church to Monroe.

November 8. John Taylor to Monroe.

1810.

February 10. John Taylor to Monroe.

  25. Monroe to Richard Brent.

March 12. John Taylor to Monroe.

June 15.   "   "

August 28. John Randolph to Monroe.

September 10. Monroe to John Taylor.

October	26.	John Taylor to Monroe.
November	13.	Henry Clay to Monroe.
	19.	Monroe to John Taylor.
	25.	John Taylor to Monroe.
December	24.	Monroe to Thomas Jefferson.
	30.	Littleton Waller Tazewell to Monroe.

1811.

January	12.	Charles Johnson to Monroe.
	14.	Monroe to Charles Johnson.
	14.	John Randolph to Monroe.
	15.	" "
	21.	Monroe to Thomas Jefferson.
	23.	Monroe to John Taylor.
	25	Thomas Jefferson to Monroe.
	31.	John Taylor to Monroe.
February	4.	Monroe to John Randolph.
	6.	Monroe to Littleton Waller Tazewell.
	13.	Monroe to John Randolph.
	13.	Littleton Waller Tazewell to Monroe.
	25.	Monroe to Littleton Waller Tazewell.
March	2.	John Randolph to Monroe.
	10?	Richard Brent to Monroe.
	17.	Littleton Waller Tazewell to Monroe.
	18.	Monroe to Richard Brent.
	18.	" "
	21.	John Taylor to Monroe.
	23.	Monroe to James Madison.
	24.	Littleton Waller Tazewell to Monroe.

March	**24.**	John Taylor to Monroe.
	29.	Monroe to James Madison.
	31.	James Madison to Monroe.
	—.	James Madison to Monroe.
April	**1.**	Richard Brent to Monroe.
	14.	Joshua Barney to Monroe.
May	**1.**	James P. Preston to Monroe.
	1.	Thomas Sumter, jr., to Monroe.
	5.	Thomas Jefferson to Monroe.
	9.	James Wilkinson to Monroe.
	10.	Littleton Waller Tazewell to Monroe.
	23.	Thomas Jefferson to Monroe.
June	**1.**	James Bowdoin to Monroe.
	3.	Monroe to John Adams.
	6.	Nicholas Biddle to Monroe.
July	**2.**	James Madison to Monroe.
	3.	Augustus John Foster to Monroe.
	12.	Joseph Fenwick to Monroe.
	23.	Monroe to Augustus John Foster.
	24.	Augustus John Foster to Monroe.
	27.	John Taylor to Monroe.
August	**7.**	John Graham to Monroe.
	11.	James Madison to Monroe.
	14.	John Graham to Monroe.
September	**4.**	'' ''
	6.	
	26.	Mathew Lyon to Monroe.
November	**8.**	Benjamin Rush to Monroe.

November **25.** Monroe to Alexander James Dallas.

25. Monroe to José Alvarez de Toledo.

30. John Winthrop to Monroe.

December **8.** Walter Jones to Monroe.

12. Benjamin Watkins Leigh to Monroe.

13. Monroe to ———.

19. John Adams to Monroe.

22. Pierce Butler to Monroe.

25. George William Erving to Monroe.

26. George Graham to Monroe.

—. Monroe to Lord Auckland.

1812.

January **2.** John Taylor to Monroe.

11. Thomas Jefferson to Monroe.

17. Littleton Waller Tazewell to Monroe.

22. John Guerrant to Monroe.

February **20.** William Tudor, jr., to Monroe.

March **12.** John Taylor to Monroe.

15. Henry Clay to Monroe.

April **2.** William Harris Crawford to Monroe.

7. Hugh Nelson to Monroe.

May **7.** John Adams to Monroe.

10. John Taylor to Monroe.

13. Monroe to John Taylor.

June **18.** John Taylor to Monroe.

21. William Wirt to Monroe.

25. John Marshall to Monroe.

July **6.** C—— Tait to Monroe.

July	13.	James Barbour to Monroe.
	29.	Henry Clay to Monroe.
August	6.	William Harris Crawford to Monroe.
	8.	James Madison to Monroe
	12.	Henry Clay to Monroe.
	23.	James Madison to Monroe.
	24.	Elbridge Gerry to Monroe.
	25.	Henry Clay to Monroe.
	28.	John Graham to Monroe.
	31.	'' ''
September	1.	James Barbour to Monroe.
	1.	James Madison to Monroe.
	4.	Monroe to ———
	4.	Richard Rush to Monroe.
	5.	James Madison to Monroe.
	6.	''
	7.	John Graham to Monroe.
	9.	William Harris Crawford to Monroe.
	10.	James Madison to Monroe.
	11.	James Barbour to Monroe.
	21.	James Madison to Monroe.
	21.	Henry Clay to Monroe.
	22.	George Hay to Monroe.
	23.	James Madison to Monroe.
	27.	John Graham to Monroe.
October	11.	John Minor to Monroe.
	22.	Richard Rush to Monroe.
	25.	Col. ——— Zuilike to Monroe.

October   **31.** George Izard to Monroe.

November   **3.** Thomas Jefferson to Monroe.

          8. John Taylor to Monroe.

          23. John Adams to Monroe.

December   **3.** Monroe to William Harris Crawford.

          18. Nicholas Biddle to Monroe.

          22. Burwell Bassett to Monroe.

          23. Monroe to George Washington Campbell.

          —. James Madison to Monroe.

          —. Thomas Paine. `` Observations on the Construction and operation of Navies—with a Plan for an Invasion of England and the final overthrow of the English Government."

1813.

January   **3.** John Francis Mercer to Monroe.

          3. George Izard to Monroe.

          4. Albert Gallatin to Monroe.

          4. Jonathan Russell to Monroe.

          15. Lewis Cass to Monroe.

February   **9.** William Eustis to Monroe.

          9. Constant Freeman to John Armstrong.   [Extract.]

          15. Monroe to John Adams.

          23. John Adams to Monroe.

          25. Monroe to James Madison.

March   **2.** David Humphreys to Monroe.

          4. Robert B. Taylor to Constant Freeman.

          4. Constant Freeman to Robert B. Taylor.

          4. Robert B. Taylor to James Barbour.

          4. Constant Freeman to James Barbour.

March 6. Andrew J. McConnico to James Barbour.

9. James Barbour to Robert B. Taylor.

9. James Barbour to Constant Freeman.

9. James Barbour. General Orders.

9. James Barbour to Charles Fenton Mercer and John Campbell.

12. J—— Preston to Monroe.

17. Nicholas Biddle to Monroe.

18. John Taylor to Monroe.

April 10. Monroe to Mrs. John Adams.

15. Monroe to Albert Gallatin, John Quincy Adams, and James Asheton Bayard.

19. Monroe to John Adams.

20. Abigail Adams to Monroe.

23. John Adams to Monroe.

29. Albert Gallatin to Monroe.

May 1.   "   "

2.   "

2.

2. Pierce Butler to Monroe.

5. Monroe to Albert Gallatin.

5. James Asheton Bayard to Monroe.

6. Monroe to James Asheton Bayard.

8. Albert Gallatin to Monroe.

14. Pierce Butler to Monroe.

30. Thomas Jefferson to Monroe.

30. William Jones to Monroe.

June 7. Monroe to Thomas Jefferson.

12. William Harris Crawford to Monroe.

15.   "   "

June   **19.**   Thomas Jefferson to Monroe.

    21.   John Francis Mercer to Monroe.

July   **8.**   Felix Grundy to Monroe.

    19.   John Graham to Monroe.

    19.   James Madison to Monroe.

    20.   John Armstrong to Monroe.

    21.   Benjamin Waterhouse to Monroe.

    22.   Alexander Baring to Albert Gallatin.

18 30.   John Quincy Adams, Albert Gallatin, and James Asheton Bayard to Count de Romanzoff.

July   **21.** } Count de Romanzoff to John Quincy Adams, Albert
August   **2.** }   Gallatin, and James Asheton Bayard.

July   **22.** } John Quincy Adams, Albert Gallatin, and James
August   **3.** }   Asheton Bayard to Count de Romanzoff.

July   **24.** } Count de Romanzoff to John Quincy Adams, Albert
August   **5.** }   Gallatin, and James Asheton Bayard. [With inclosure.]

August   **2 14.**   "Inofficial Notes concerning the Impressment of Seamen on board of American Vessels, by the Officers of the British Navy."

    5.   Monroe to Albert Gallatin.

    8.   James Wilkinson to Monroe.

    15.   James Madison to Monroe.

    19.   "   "

    20.   "

    22.

    24.   William Shaler to Monroe.

15 27.   Albert Gallatin to Alexander Baring.

17/29.   Albert Gallatin, John Quincy Adams, and James Asheton Bayard to Monroe.

    28.   Albert Gallatin to Monroe.

September   **1.**   James Madison to Monroe.

      2.   "   "

      7.   J—— B—— Colvin to Monroe.

      13.   Daniel Brent to Monroe.

      18.   James Madison to Monroe.

      18.   Willie Blount to James Madison. [Extract in the writing of Madison sent to Monroe.]

      23.   James Madison to Monroe.

      27.   John Graham to Monroe.

      30.   James Wilkinson to Monroe.

October   **3 15.**   Albert Gallatin, John Quincy Adams, and James Asheton Bayard to Monroe.

      .5.   Albert Gallatin to Monroe.

      17.   James Madison to Monroe.

      18.   "   "

November   **12.**   George Washington Campbell to Monroe.

      22.   John Quincy Adams to ——· Speyer. [Extract.]

      23.   Levett Harris to —— Speyer.

December   **6.**   John Taylor to Monroe.

      27.   Monroe to James Madison.

      —.   Monroe.   Notes relative to expedition against Canada.

      —.   James Madison to Monroe.

      —.   Albert Gallatin.   "Local force" of the U. S. Army, Number and distribution, Organization and expense.

      —.   Albert Gallatin.   Notes relative to General Harrison's expedition.

      —.   Albert Gallatin to Monroe.

1814.

January	**18.**	Alexander James Dallas to Monroe.
	19.	" " " "
	27.	Thomas Jefferson to Monroe.
February	**2.**	Jeremiah Morrow to Monroe.
	6.	Jonathan Russell to Monroe.
	10.	Monroe to Jonathan Russell.
	11.	" " " "
	13.	Henry Clay to Monroe.
	14.	Monroe to the Governors of Louisiana and the Mississippi Territory.
	14.	Henry Clay to Monroe.
	17.	Monroe to Tully Robinson.
	17.	Monroe to William C. C. Claiborne.
	18.	Monroe to Henry Clay.
	23.	Henry Clay to Monroe.
March	**2.**	John Adams to William Stephens Smith.
	2.	William Wyatt Bibb to Monroe.
	4.	John Adams to William Stephens Smith.
	27.	Chevalier de Onis to Monroe.
April	**23.**	Henry Clay to Monroe.
	30.	Daniel Brent to Monroe.
	30.	John Jacob Astor to Monroe.
	—.	Monroe to ———.
	—.	Monroe. Notes on the restoration of peace with Great Britain.
May	**1.**	James Madison to Monroe.
	2.	David Parish to Alexander James Dallas.
	3.	Alexander James Dallas to Monroe.

May

6. James Asheton Bayard and Albert Gallatin to Monroe.

7. Charles Jared Ingersoll to Monroe.

7. James Madison to Monroe.

9. R—— G—— Beasley to Monroe.

12. James Madison to Monroe.

13. R—— G—— Beasley to Monroe.

13. George Washington Campbell to Monroe.

14. Monroe to James Madison.

16.   ' '   " "

19. James Madison to Monroe.

21.   "   "

23.

24. John Jacob Astor to Monroe.

26. Andrew Jackson to John Williams.

26. James Madison to Monroe.

June

1. John Jacob Astor to Monroe.

3. James Madison to Monroe.

8. Charles Jared Ingersoll to Monroe.

25. Monroe to William Harris Crawford.

30. Charles Jared Ingersoll to Monroe.

July

3. Monroe to ————.

11. Elbridge Gerry to Monroe.

14. James Madison to Monroe.

14. John Graham to Monroe.

15. John Armstrong to Monroe.

18. James Trimble to Alexander James Dallas.

27. Alexander James Dallas to William Jones. [With inclosures.]

July   —. Monroe. Notes relative to the burning of Washington.

August   1. Philip Key to Monroe.

3. Thomas Jefferson to Monroe.

7. Henry Clay. Extract from journal.

11. James Brown to Monroe.

12. John Wayles Eppes to Monroe.

14. William Pinkney to Monroe.

18. Monroe to John Armstrong.

18. Henry Clay to Monroe.

18. John Armstrong to Monroe.

20. William Henry Winder to James Madison.

21. Monroe to James Madison.

21?

21. James Madison to Monroe.

28. John Smith to Edward Tiffin.

29. George Graham to William Henry Winder.

29. B—— Oden to William Henry Winder.

—. Monroe to James Madison.

September 1. Joseph Hopper Nicholson to Monroe.

2. John Jacob Astor to Monroe.

3. Monroe to James Madison.

4. Henry St. George Tucker to Monroe.

5. Monroe to Andrew Jackson.

5. William Jones to James Madison.

5. Morgan Lewis to Monroe.

7. Alexander James Dallas to Monroe.

8. Monroe to James Madison.

September **11.** Morgan Lewis to Monroe.

12. Paul Bentalou to Monroe.

18. George Izard to Monroe.

18. Joseph Hopper Nicholson to Monroe.

20. Lewis Cass to Monroe.

24. Paul Bentalou to Monroe.

25. Monroe to Willie Blount, governor of Tennessee.

25. Monroe to Peter Early, governor of Georgia.

25. Monroe to James Madison.

25. Jonathan Russell to Albert Gallatin.

27. Monroe to Andrew Jackson.

29. Thomas Lloyd to Monroe.

—. Monroe to James Madison.

October **1.** James Brown to Monroe.

3. Monroe to Willie Blount, governor of Tennessee.

3. Monroe to Isaac Shelby, governor of Kentucky.

10. Monroe to Peter Early, governor of Georgia.

10. Monroe to Willie Blount, governor of Tennessee.

10. Monroe to Andrew Jackson.

10. Monroe to Isaac Shelby, governor of Kentucky.

15. Monroe to Morgan Lewis.

16. Thomas Jefferson to Monroe.

17. Marinus Willett to Monroe.

19. G—— S—— Smith to William Harris Crawford.

21. Monroe to Andrew Jackson.

26. Henry Clay to Monroe.

26. Albert Gallatin to Monroe.

26. Andrew Jackson to Monroe.

October	**26.**	Jonathan Russell to Monroe.
	28.	Monroe to Isaac Shelby, governor of Kentucky.
	31.	Andrew Jackson to Monroe.
November	**—.**	James Brown to Monroe.
	3.	Monroe to Willie Blount, governor of Tennessee.
	3.	Monroe to Isaac Shelby, governor of Kentucky.
	4.	Monroe to Willie Blount, governor of Tennessee.
	10.	United States Peace Commissioners. "Extract of a letter . . . to the British."
	20.	George Izard to Monroe.
	25.	John Mullowny to Monroe.
December	**4.**	George William Erving to Monroe.
	5.	" "
	7.	Monroe to Andrew Jackson.
	10.	Monroe to Peter Early, governor of Georgia.
	10.	Monroe to Andrew Jackson.
	10.	Walter Jones to Monroe.
	16.	William Harris Crawford to Monroe.
	17.	Alexander James Dallas to Monroe.
	19.	William Harris Crawford to Monroe.
	21.	Monroe to Thomas Jefferson.
	21.	William Harris Crawford to Monroe.
	22.	Henry Brockholst Livingston to Monroe.
	25.	Henry Clay to Monroe.
	25.	Jonathan Russell to Monroe.
	26.	Comte de Goltz to William Harris Crawford.
	28.	William Harris Crawford to Monroe.
	28.	" "

December **29.** William Harris Crawford to Comte de Goltz.

29. William Harris Crawford to the consuls of the United States. [Circular.]

30. William Harris Crawford to Monroe.

—. Monroe to the Military Committee of the Senate.

—. Monroe. Notes respecting the rejection by Great Britain of the mediation of Russia.

—. Monroe to William Harris Crawford.

—. Anonymous. Notes relative to expedition against Canada.

—. John Wayles Eppes to Monroe.

1815.

January **1.** Thomas Jefferson to Monroe.

6. George Hay to Monroe.

14. Lancelot Minor to Thomas Jefferson. [With inclosures.]

19. Anthony Morris to George William Erving.

26. Samuel Shaw to Monroe.

26. Anthony Morris to George William Erving.

27. Wilson Cary Nicholas to Monroe.

27. George William Erving to Monroe.

30. Anthony Morris to George William Erving.

30. Monroe to Willie Blount, governor of Tennessee.

30. Monroe to Isaac Shelby, governor of Kentucky.

—. Benjamin Williams Crowninshield. Articles 3, 4, and 5 of the proposed treaty with Great Britain.

February —. Monroe to the chairman of the Military Committee of the Senate.

3. George William Erving to Anthony Morris.

5. Monroe to Andrew Jackson.

February   10.   Monroe to Isaac Shelby, governor of Kentucky.

10.   George William Erving to Anthony Morris.

12.   George William Erving to Monroe.   [With inclosures.]

13.   Monroe to Willie Blount, governor of Tennessee.

13.   Monroe to Peter Early, governor of Georgia.

13.   Monroe to Andrew Jackson.

13.   Monroe to Isaac Shelby, governor of Kentucky.

14.   Monroe to Peter Early, governor of Georgia.

14.   Monroe to Willie Blount, governor of Tennessee.

14.   Monroe to Isaac Shelby, governor of Kentucky.

15.   George Hay to Monroe.

16.   Monroe to Andrew Jackson.

20.   William Harris Crawford to Monroe.

20.   "   ".

21.

22.   Monroe to the chairman of the Military Committee of the Senate.

22.   Alexander James Dallas to Monroe.

25.   William Harris Crawford to Monroe.

26.   Jonathan Russell to Monroe.

28.   George William Erving to Monroe.   [With inclosures.]

March   1.   Jonathan Dayton to Monroe.

2.   Richard Butler.   Extract of general orders.

2.   John Minor to Monroe.

3.   John Pleasants, jr., to Monroe.

6.   Thomas L. L. Brent to George William Erving.

7.   William Harris Crawford to Jaucourt.

March   **7.** Jaucourt to William Harris Crawford.

       8.   "   "

       8. William Harris Crawford to Monroe.

       9. William Harris Crawford to Jancourt.

       9.   "   "

      13. Alexander James Dallas to Monroe.

      16. William Harris Crawford to Monroe.

      16.   "   "

      16.

      16.

      19. Jancourt to William Harris Crawford.   [With inclosure.]

      19. William Eustis to Monroe.

      19. William Harris Crawford to Monroe.

      19.   "   "

      21.

      21.

      21.

      21. Charles Scott Todd to Anthony Butler

      22. George Logan to Monroe.

      26. James Madison to Monroe.

      27.   "   "

      29.

      —.

April   **2.** St. George Tucker to Monroe.

      3. Monroe to James Madison.

      4. James Madison to Monroe.

      5.   "   "

April   5.   Anthony Butler to Gordon Drummond.

6.   James Madison to Monroe.

8.   "   "

9.

10.   Monroe to William Shaler, William Bainbridge, and Stephen Decatur.

10.   James Madison to Monroe.

15.   ..   "

18.

23.

24.

25.   Monroe to James Madison.

25.   James Madison to Monroe.

26.   Jean Matthieu Philibert Serurier to Monroe.

27.   George Murray to Anthony Butler.

27.   Alexander James Dallas to Monroe.

28.   Christopher Hughes, jr., to Monroe.

28.   James Madison to Monroe.

30.   Monroe to ———.

May   1.   Asbury Dickins to James Madison.

2.   James Madison to Monroe.

4.   "   "

5.   Monroe to James Madison.

8.   Anthony Butler to Monroe.

10.   James Madison to Monroe.

11.   Monroe to Albert Gallatin.

18.   James Madison to Monroe.

26.   John Taylor to Monroe.

May	28.	Monroe to Alexander James Dallas.
	28.	Alexander James Dallas to Monroe.
	30.	James Madison to Monroe.
	31.	Alexander James Dallas to Anthony Butler.
June	1.	John Church Hamilton to Monroe.
	1.	Alexander James Dallas to Monroe.
	12.	James Madison to Monroe.
	14.	" "
	15.	Richard Rush to Monroe.
	26.	James Madison to Monroe.
July	8.	Alexander James Dallas to Monroe.
	9.	George Hay to Monroe.
	15.	Thomas Jefferson to Monroe.
	15.	Alexander James Dallas to Monroe.
	19.	Eleazar Wheelock Ripley to Monroe.
	20.	Joel Roberts Poinsett to Monroe.
	25.	Pierre Samuel Du Pont de Nemours to Monroe.
	31.	James Madison to Monroe.
August	2.	William Pinkney to Monroe.
	5.	James Madison to Monroe.
	7.	Richard Rush to Monroe.
	9.	" "
	9.	James Madison to Monroe.
	10.	" "
	14.	
September	9.	Richard Rush to Monroe.
	12.	James Madison to Monroe.
	17.	Richard Rush to James Madison.

September 28. John Graham to Monroe.

29. James Madison to Monroe.

October 11. George William Erving to Monroe.

12. George Washington Campbell to Monroe.

16. William Harris Crawford to Monroe.

20. William Pinkney to Monroe.

27. Anthony Morris to Monroe.   [With inclosures.]

November 16. John Mercer to Monroe.

23. Albert Gallatin to Monroe.

25.

29. Littleton Waller Tazewell to Monroe.   [With inclosure.]

30. Albert Gallatin to Monroe.   [With inclosure.]

December 3. John Taylor to Monroe.

14. Monroe to W—— Marbury.

16. Monroe to Albert Gallatin.

26. Albert Gallatin to Monroe.

29. Pierre Samuel Du Pont de Nemours to Monroe.

31. Jean Matthieu Philibert Serurier to Monroe.

1816.

January 13. George William Erving to Monroe.

19. Monroe to Luis de Onis.

February 18. David Rogerson Williams to Monroe.

24. George William Erving to Monroe.

March 2. Joseph Hopper Nicholson to Monroe.

4. Alexander James Dallas to Monroe.

18. George William Erving to Monroe.

—. William Pinkney to Monroe.

March   **19.** Samuel Smith and Richard Mentor Johnson to Monroe.

       19.   "

       21. Pierre Samuel Du Pont de Nemours to Monroe.

       21. Christopher Hughes, jr., to Monroe.

       23. George William Erving to Monroe.

       25. Peter Buel Porter to Monroe.

April   **13.** Christopher Hughes, jr., to Monroe.

       14. Henry Jackson to Monroe.

May   **8.** Andrew Jackson to Monroe.

       12.   "   "

       23. Jean Matthieu Philibert Serurier to Monroe.

June   **1.** Albert Gallatin to Monroe.

       2. William Pinkney to Monroe.

       13. James Madison to Monroe.

       15. John McLean to Monroe.

       17. Peter Stephen Du Ponceau to Monroe.

       24. James Madison to Monroe.

       25.   "   "

       27. Monroe to James Madison.

       27. Monroe to Peter Stephen Du Ponceau.

July   **2.** Peter Stephen Du Ponceau to Monroe.

       2. James Madison to Monroe.

       5. Luis de Onis to Monroe.

       5. Peter Stephen Du Ponceau?. Extract of "Jackson's account of the Empire of Morocco," page 180.

       6. Christopher Hughes, jr., to Monroe.

       7. Monroe to James Madison.

       8. James Madison to Monroe.

July	9.	Andrew Jackson to Monroe.
	11.	James Madison to Monroe.
	15.	" "
	19.	
	20.	Peter Stephen Du Ponceau to Monroe.
	21.	James Madison to Monroe.
	27.	Andrew Jackson to Monroe.
August	21.	John Graham to Monroe.
	24.	" "
	28.	
	29.	Thomas Jefferson to Monroe.
September	1.	John Graham to Monroe.
	5.	George Washington Campbell to Monroe.
	10.	John Graham to Monroe.
	13.	" "
	22.	George William Erving to Monroe.
	15.	—— Vincent to Monroe.
	15.	John Graham to Monroe.
	27.	Pierce Butler to Monroe.
October	7.	William Pinkney to Monroe.
	11.	George William Erving to Monroe.
	16.	Jean Matthieu Philibert Serurier to Monroe.
	21.	Richard Rush to Monroe.
	29.	August de Nagell to Monroe.
November	7.	William Eustis to Monroe.
	12.	Pierce Butler to Monroe.
December	14.	Monroe to Andrew Jackson.
	15.	John Clarke to Monroe.

December **15.** Geoige William Eiving to Monioe.

17. John Adams to Monroe.

25. George William Eiving to José Pizairo.

26. William Eustis to Monioe.

26.   "   "

26. Geoige William Eiving to Monioe.

1817.

January **31.** William Pinkney to Monioe.

February **5.** Pieiie Samuel DuPont de Nemouis to Monioe.

9. Thomas Todd to Monioe.

20. Monroe to Isaac Shelby, goveinor of Kentucky.

22. William Tudoi, jr., to Monioe.

26. Pieiie Samuel DuPont de Nemouis to Monroe.

March **2.** George William Erving to Monioe.

3. John Giaham to George Giaham.

6. Monroe to John Quincy Adams.

17. Monroe to George Mifflin Dallas.

29. John Adams to William Tudor.

April **1.** Richard Rush to Monroe.

8. Thomas Jefferson to Monroe.

12. Theodoie Lyman, jr., to Monioe.

13. Thomas Jefferson to Monioe.

14. Rufus King to Monioe.

24. Richaid Rush to Monioe.

29. Monroe to Rufus King.

May **2.** William Haiiis Crawford to Monroe.

5. John Biooks to Monioe.

6. John Quincy Adams to Monioe.

May   6. Cæsaι Augustus Rodney to Monιoe.

7. Joel Robeιts Poinsett to Monιoe.

June   3. Richaιd Rush to Monιoe.

3.   ''   ''

4.

4. James Bιown to Monιoe.

5. Richaιd Rush to Monιoe.

5. Geoιge Logan to Monιoe.

⌐ 6. Cæsaι Augustus Rodney to Monιoe.

7. Richaιd Rush to Monιoe.

8. Cæsaι Augustus Rodney to Monroe.

9. Jonathan Russell to Monιoe.

10. Chaιles Robeιt, Count von Nesselιode to Monιoe.

11. Richaιd Rush to Monιoe.

11. William Tudoι, jr., to Monroe.

13. Richard Rush to Monroe.

14.   "   "

19. John Adams to Monιoe.

21, Richaιd Rush to Monιoe.

21.   ''   ''

10 22. William Pinkney to Monιoe.

25. Richaιd Rush to Monroe.

26.   ''   ''

27.

27. John Adams to Monιoe.

28. Richaιd Rush to Monιoe.

July   10. Geoιge Sullivan to Monroe.

11. William Tudor to Monroe.

July	13.	Richard Rush to Monroe.
	16.	" "
	17.	
	18.	Albert Gallatin to Monroe. [With inclosure.]
	20.	Monroe to Thomas Sumter.
	20.	Richard Rush to Monroe.
	27.	" "
	28.	
August	21.	John Quincy Adams to Monroe.
	22.	James Madison to Monroe.
	24.	Richard Rush to Monroe.
September	3.	William Eustis to Monroe.
	6.	Luis de Onis to R. Rush, Acting Secretary of State.
	9.	Cæsar Augustus Rodney to Monroe.
	12.	John McLean to Monroe.
	16.	Walter & Miller to John Quincy Adams.
	17.	Edward St. Loe Livermore to Monroe.
	19.	Luis de Onis to Richard Rush, Acting Secretary of State.
	22.	Richard Rush to Monroe.
	23.	" "
	25.	
	26.	
	27.	William Lee to John Quincy Adams.
	27.	John Quincy Adams to Monroe.
	28.	Richard Rush to Monroe.
	29.	John Quincy Adams to James Trecothic Austin.
	30.	Richard Rush to Monroe.

October   1.   William Harris Crawford to Monroe.

1.   Richard Rush to Monroe.

2.   "   "

3.   John Quincy Adams to Monroe.

3.   André Daschkoff to John Quincy Adams.

4.   John Quincy Adams to Monroe.

4.   Richard Rush to Monroe.

6.   John Quincy Adams to Monroe.

7.   "   "

8.

11.   William Harris Crawford to Monroe.

13.   Thomas Jefferson to Monroe.

17.   Richard Rush to Monroe.

21.   James Madison to Monroe.

25.   Anonymous. "A Memoir concerning the acquisitions of territory and population, by Great Britain, in India."

26.   George Hay to Monroe.   [Incomplete.]

31.   Cæsar Augustus Rodney to Monroe.

—.   Monroe.   Questions submitted to his Cabinet.

November   1.   Richard Rush to Monroe.

1.   John Caldwell Calhoun to Monroe.

3.   De Witt Clinton to Monroe.

5.   Cæsar Augustus Rodney to Monroe.

8.   William Wirt to Monroe.

11.   Cæsar Augustus Rodney to Monroe.

15.   Richard Rush to Monroe.

15.   Theodorick Bland to Monroe.

November   22. Richard Rush to Monroe.

23.   "   "

26.

29. James Madison to Monroe.

December   9.   "

11. Nicholas Biddle to Monroe.

12. José Miguel de Carrera to H—— Disdier.

12. Anonymous.   Letter from Santiago de Chili.

14.   "   "   "

17. Richard Rush to Monroe.

25.   "   "

27. James Madison to Monroe.

—. Monroe to ——— Lyman.

—. Monroe.   Notes relative to military matters.

—. Anonymous.   "The Political Picture of Europe in 1817."

—. Edmund Burke to ———.   [Extract in hand of Richard Rush.]

—. William Peter Van Ness.   Extract from memorial relative to revision of the rules of the prize court.

1818.

January   4. William Harris Crawford to Monroe.

6. Richard Rush to Monroe.

11. Anonymous.   "Inclosed in Nich. Biddle's letters to Mr. Monroe."

17. Oliver Wolcott to Josiah Meigs.

21. William Pinkney to Monroe.

24. Richard Rush to Monroe.

—. Notes relative to letter of Nicholas Biddle.

January   —.   William Harris Crawford to Monroe.

         —.   "

February   **7.**   Nicholas Biddle to Monroe.

         8.   Cæsar Augustus Rodney to Monroe.

         18.   James Madison to Monroe.

         19.   Richard Rush to Monroe.

         25.   Nicholas Biddle to Monroe.

         28.   William Wirt to Monroe.

March   **4.**   David Porter to Monroe.

         4.   Cæsar Augustus Rodney to Monroe.

         5.   Nicholas Biddle to Monroe.

         5.   John Graham to Monroe.

         15.   Nicholas Biddle to Monroe.

         17.   Joseph Codina to Monroe.   [With inclosure.]

         22.   Nicholas Biddle to Monroe.

         23.   William Harris Crawford to Monroe.

         24.   Richard Rush to Monroe.

         25.   John Quincy Adams to Monroe.

April   **10.**   Bernard Germain Etienne de la Ville, Comte de Lacépède, to Monroe.

         11.   James Biddle to Nicholas Biddle.

         14.   Theodorick Bland to Monroe.

         22.   Richard Rush to Monroe.

         22.   Charles Jared Ingersoll to Monroe.

         24.   Cæsar Augustus Rodney to Monroe.

         25.   Richard Rush to Monroe.

         —.   Monroe.   Notes relative to tariff.

         —.   Monroe.   Notes respecting navigation, British ports, etc.

April	—.	Monroe. Project for the proposed navigation laws between Great Britain and the United States.
May	**10.**	Richard Rush to Monroe. [With inclosures.]
	20.	" "
	21.	James Madison to Monroe.
	25.	Richard Rush to Monroe.
	30.	" "
June	**3.**	Cæsar Augustus Rodney to Monroe.
	5.	Richard Rush to Monroe.
	25.	Marc Antoine Jullien de Paris to Monroe.
	29.	Rufus King to Monroe.
	29.	Richard Rush to Monroe.
July	**9.**	" "
	19.	Charles Jared Ingersoll to Monroe.
	21.	Richard Rush to Monroe.
	28.	James Yard to Monroe.
	28.	Mountjoy Bayly to Monroe.
August	**12.**	John Quincy Adams to Monroe.
	13.	Richard Rush to Monroe.
	13.	John Quincy Adams to Monroe.
	17.	Monroe to John Quincy Adams.
	18.	Richard Rush to Monroe.
	20.	Monroe to John Quincy Adams.
	20.	Christopher Hughes, jr., to Monroe.
	20.	John Quincy Adams to Monroe.
	20.	William Eustis to Monroe.
August **October**	**20–** **20.**	Richard Rush. "Notes of the joint negotiation at London."

August   22. John Caldwell Calhoun to Monroe.

23. John Quincy Adams to Monroe.

24.   "   "

25. Richard Rush to Monroe.

27. Monroe to John Quincy Adams.

29. John Caldwell Calhoun to Monroe.

—. James Madison to Monroe.

September   3. John Caldwell Calhoun. "Statement in the case of Lieutenant McLeod."

4. John Caldwell Calhoun to Monroe.

6. Richard Rush to Monroe.

6. John Caldwell Calhoun to Monroe.

17. Thomas Jefferson to Monroe.

19. John Caldwell Calhoun to Monroe.

25. Richard Rush to Monroe.

28. Nicholas Biddle to Monroe.

October   1. Richard Rush to Monroe.

2. James Madison to Monroe.

6. Lewis Cass to Monroe.

17. Richard Rush to Monroe.

22.   "   "

November   1.

4. Theodorick Bland to Monroe.

4. Cæsar Augustus Rodney to Monroe.

4.   "   "

7. Albert Gallatin to John Quincy Adams.

10. Richard Rush to Monroe.

21.   "   "

November **22.** Charles Jared Ingersoll to Monroe.

23. James Madison to Monroe.

30. Monroe.   Message to the Senate.

—. Monroe to Luis de Onis.

December **11.** James Madison to Monroe.

14. Oliver Wolcott to Monroe.

20. Thomas Bolling Robertson to Monroe.

—. Monroe.   Memorandum for Secretary of War and Navy.

—. "A British Merchant" to Richard Rush?

1819.

January **3.** David Porter to Monroe.

6. John Connelly to Jonathan Roberts.

10. Solomon P. Sharp to Monroe.

12. Jonathan Roberts to Monroe.

17. Richard Rush to Monroe.

18. Samuel Delucenna Ingham to Jonathan Roberts.

18. Nicholas Biddle to Monroe.

24. Jonathan Roberts to Monroe.

24. Nicholas Biddle to Monroe.

31.   " "   "

February **7.** Monroe to James Madison.

7. Nicholas Biddle to Monroe.

10. Richard Rush to Monroe.

10. John Wayles Eppes to Monroe.

12. Benjamin Waterhouse to John Quincy Adams.

12. George Hay to Monroe.

13. James Madison to Monroe.

February	**13.**	James Miller to Monroe.
	14.	Cæsar Augustus Rodney to Monroe.
	20.	Monroe to John Adams.
	21.	L. M. La Revelliere-Lépeaux to Monroe.
March	**1.**	Mrs. Maria Dallas to Monroe.
	1.	Nicholas Biddle to Monroe.
	1.	Warden Pope to Monroe.
	2.	Lewis Cass to Monroe.
	3.	Jonathan Roberts to Monroe.
	7.	Monroe to Richard Rush.
	17.	Donatien Le Ray de Chaumont to Monroe.
	18.	George de Silverhjelm to Monroe.
	20.	George Washington Campbell to Monroe.
	20.	Cæsar Augustus Rodney to Monroe.
	21.	Richard Mentor Johnson to Monroe.
	24.	Monroe. Sketch of instructions for agent for South America. Notes for the Department of State.
	—.	Monroe to John Quincy Adams.
April	**7.**	William Harris Crawford to Monroe.
	17.	Daniel Stevens to Monroe.
	24.	John Geddes to Monroe.
	24.	William Roach, jr., to Monroe.
	24.	Morton A. Waring to Monroe.
May	**1.**	Charles Henry Du Pasquier to Monroe.
	2.	George Hay to Monroe.
	2.	James Lloyd to William Lee.
	15.	George Washington Campbell to Monroe.
	23.	Monroe to Andrew Jackson.

May   —. William Harris Crawford to Monroe.

June   6. Cæsar Augustus Rodney to ———.

            —. John Henry Eaton to Monroe.

            7. Nashville Committee of Citizens to Monroe.

            8. —— Terrien to "James Madison, President des Etats Unis."

            8. —— Terrien to Martin Du Colombier.

            12. James Lloyd to William Lee.

            26. Monroe to John Quincy Adams.

            30.   "   "

July   2. William Harris Crawford to Monroe.

            3. James Madison to Monroe.

            5. Nicholas Biddle to Monroe.

            11. Richard Mentor Johnson to Monroe.

            17. Richard Rush to Monroe.

            21. Nicholas Biddle to Monroe.

            21? Donatien Le Ray de Chaumont to Monroe.

            24. Monroe to John Quincy Adams.

August   3.   "   "

            4. John Quincy Adams to Monroe.

            17. Richard Rush to Monroe.

            19. William Wirt to Monroe.

            20. William Irving to Monroe.

            20. William Pinkney to Monroe.

            30. Pierce Butler to Monroe.

September 1. John Graham to John Quincy Adams.

            4. Monroe to John Quincy Adams.

            5. John Caldwell Calhoun to Monroe.

            6. Benjamin Homans to Monroe.

September   **8.** John Caldwell Calhoun to Monroe.

           8. Smith Thompson to Benjamin Homans.

         10. Benjamin Homans to Monroe.

         10.   "   "

         14. John Caldwell Calhoun to Monroe.

         15. Albert Gallatin to Monroe.

         17. Benjamin Homans to Monroe.

         17. Rufus King to Monroe.

         25. Richard Rush to Monroe.

         30. Cæsar Augustus Rodney to Monroe.

October   **1.** Benjamin Homans to Monroe.

          2. Charles Jared Ingersoll to Monroe.

          3. Benjamin Homans to Monroe.

          5. Levett Harris to Monroe.

          5. William Wirt to Monroe.

          6. Richard Cutts to Monroe.

          7. Benjamin Homans to Monroe.

          9.   "   "

         23. William Eustis to Monroe.

         31. John Graham to Monroe.

November **3.** John Adams to Monroe.

         11. John Holmes to Monroe.

         15. Monroe to Thomas Jefferson.

         16. Monroe to James Madison.

         16. Andrew Jackson to Monroe.

         17. Christopher Vandeventer to Monroe.

         17. Daniel Parker. Disposition of the United States troops on the southern seaboard and inland stations of the seventh and eighth departments.

November **28.** Tench Coxe to Monroe.   [With enclosure.]

29. Alexander McRae to Monroe.

December **4.** John Mullowny to Jonathan Roberts.

6. Anonymous.   Memorandum relative to "An Affair of Honor" between John Harris and William Lewis.

7. Richard Rush to Monroe.

7. Charles Jared Ingersoll to Monroe.

9. Nicholas Biddle to Monroe.

11. James Madison to Monroe.

11. John Mullowny to Jonathan Roberts.

15. Jonathan Roberts to Monroe.

24. George Hay to Monroe.

30. Andrew Jackson to Monroe.

—. Anonymous.   Notes on the commerce of Odessa, Constantinople,.and Smyrna.

—. Anonymous.   "Notes on the Plague."

—. Thomas Williamson to Monroe.

—. Hyde de Neuville to John Quincy Adams.

—. Abner Lacock to Monroe.

—.   "   "

1820.

January **1.** Correa de Serra to Monroe.

15. George Sullivan to Monroe.

30. Abner Lacock to Monroe.

18/30. George Washington Campbell to Monroe.

February **6.** Richard Rush to Monroe.

10. James Madison to Monroe.

12. George Hay to Monroe.

February   13. Cæsar Augustus Rodney to Monroe.

15. Geoige Hay to Monroe.

16.   "   ''

17.

22. John Quincy Adams to Chailes S. Todd.

23. James Madison to Monroe.

26. Richaid Rush to Monroe.

28. Christophei Hughes, jr., to Monroe.

March   3. Thomas Jeffeison to Monroe.

4. Cæsai Augustus Rodney to Monroe.

6. John Adams to Monroe.

20. Richaid Rush to Monroe.

. **April**   3. Cæsai Augustus Rodney to Monroe.

8. William Wirt to Monroe.

10. Mountjoy Bayly to Monroe.

14. William Pinkney to Monroe.

15. Monroe.   Notes ielative to navigation act.

24. Francisco Dionisio Vives to John Quincy Adams.

—. Monioe.   Notes ielative to South American colonies.

May   10. Richard Rush to Monroe.

June   3. John Vawtei to Jonathan Lyon.

5. Henry Deaiboin to Monroe.

8. John Quincy Adams to Monroe.

12. William Hairis Crawfoid to Monroe.   [Incomplete.]

12. United States Jurymen.   Certificates for the payment of fees.   Signed by Jonathan Lyon, J—— Haibison, and H—— Dawalt.

June   **15.** John Quincy Adams to Monroe.

          17.   "   "

          20.

          21. John Mooie.   Certificate that the maishal of Indiana refused to pay jurors of the United States district court.

          22. Richard Rush to Monroe.

          23. Jonathan Lyon, J——— Haibison, and H——— Dawalt to William Haiiis Crawfoid.

          30. John Quincy Adams to Monroe.

July   **5.** John Quincy Adams.   General instructions to Hugh Middleton.

          7. John Quincy Adams to Richard Rush.

          8. William Haıris Ciawfoid to Monroe.

          11. John Quincy Adams to Monroe.

          18.   "   "

          21. Richard Rush to Monioe.

          27.   "   "

          29. John Quincy Adams to Monioe.

          29. Joseph Anderson to William Hariis Crawford.

          29? William Harris Crawford to Monioe.

          29? Monroe.   Memorandum respecting chaiges against John Vawter, marshal of Indiana.

August   **2.** John Quincy Adams to Monioe.

          5.   "   "

          6. Richard Rush to Monroe.

          11. John Quincy Adams to Monroe.

          15.   "   "

          20. Manuel Toires to John Quincy Adams.   [Translation.]

August	**21.**	John Quincy Adams to Monroe.
	25.	"　　　　　　"
	26.	
	27	
	29.	
	29.	James Madison to Monroe.
	30.	John Quincy Adams to Monroe.
September	**1.**	"　　　　　　"
	2.	Cæsar Augustus Rodney to Monroe.
	4.	John Quincy Adams to Monroe.
	7.	"　　　　　　"
	8.	
	11.	
	11.	Baron Stoganoff to Commodore William Bainbridge. [Translation.]
	13.	John Quincy Adams to Monroe.
	15.	"　　　　　　"
	19.	Cæsar Augustus Rodney to Monroe.
	26.	John Quincy Adams to Monroe.
	27.	"　　　　　　"
	27.	
	27.	Alexander Baring to Monroe.
	29.	John Quincy Adams to Monroe.
October	**7.**	"　　　　　　"
	7.	
	11.	
	16.	Langdon Cheves to William Harris Crawford. Inclosing "A Plan of Financial Supply for the Year 1821 and subsequent Years."

November   **8.** James Madison to Monroe.

     10. Charles Scott Todd to Monroe.

     17. Cæsar Augustus Rodney to Monroe.

     19. James Madison to Monroe.

     25. Richard Rush to Monroe.

December   **8.** Archibald Stuart to Monroe.

     24. Richard Rush to Monroe.

     27. Cæsar Augustus Rodney to Monroe.

     28. James Madison to Monroe.

     —.   "   "

     —. Monroe.   Draft of a statement to be presented to the Emperor of Russia.

     —. Monroe.   Parties in Cuba.

     —. "Notes taken from a Spanish Paper for Mr. Monroe."

1821.

January   **3.** John Freedley to Jonathan Roberts.

     6. George Bomford to John Caldwell Calhoun.

     6. James Madison to Monroe.

     8. Monroe to —— Forrest.

     9. William Wirt to Monroe.

     9. William Harris Crawford to William Wirt.

     13. Cæsar Augustus Rodney to Monroe.

     18. Jonathan Roberts to Monroe.

     22. Andrew Jackson to Monroe.

     26. Nicholas Biddle to William Harris Crawford.

     28. Edward Lloyd to Monroe.

     28.   "   "

January   **29.** Nicholas Biddle to William Harris Crawford.

           29. Nicholas Biddle to Monroe.

February   **9.** Lewis Cass to Monroe.

           21. Count de Palmela.   Project of a constitution supposed to have been submitted to the King of Portugal.

           22. Thomas Pinckney to John Caldwell Calhoun.

           27. Nicholas Biddle to Monroe.

March   **2.** William Wirt to Monroe.

           2. John Quincy Adams to Monroe.

           7. Richard Rush to Monroe.

           12. John Quincy Adams.   Extracts of instructions to Andrew Jackson.

           20. John Forsyth to Monroe.

           20. Thomas Sumter, jr., to Monroe.

           26. Cæsar Augustus Rodney to Monroe.

           28. Robert Tillotson to Monroe.

           —. William Wirt to Monroe.

April   —. Abner Lacock to Monroe.

           4. Cæsar Augustus Rodney to Monroe.

           4. Richard Rush to Monroe.

           7. James Madison to Monroe.

           21. William Eustis to Monroe.

May   **4.** James Madison to Monroe.

           9. Samuel T. Anderson to Monroe.

           16. James Madison to Monroe.

           18. Eligius Fromentin.   Commission to, as United States judge for West Florida.

           20. James Wilkinson to Monroe.

May   21. Cæsar Augustus Rodney to Monroe.

             23. Monroe to Andrew Jackson.

             24. Cæsar Augustus Rodney to Monroe.

June   4. Abner Lacock to Monroe.

              5. Alexander Kerr to Monroe.

             13. Andrew Jackson to Monroe.

             14. Nicholas Biddle to Monroe.

             17. J—— S—— Monroe to Monroe.

             18. Smith Thompson to Monroe.

             18. John Caldwell Calhoun to Monroe.

             19. Smith Thompson to Monroe.

             19. John Caldwell Calhoun to Monroe.

             19.   "   "

             27. John Quincy Adams to Eligius Fromentin.

             27. Richard Rush to Monroe.

July   9. John Quincy Adams to Monroe.

             12. Monroe to John Quincy Adams.

             14. John Quincy Adams to Monroe.

             16. Smith Thompson to Monroe.

             19. John Quincy Adams to Charles Scott Todd.

             20. John Caldwell Calhoun to Monroe.

             20. William Harris Crawford to Monroe.

             23. John Quincy Adams to Monroe.

             25.   "   "

             28. John Caldwell Calhoun to Monroe.

             31. John Quincy Adams to Monroe.

             —. Monroe to John Quincy Adams.

August   1. William Harris Crawford to Monroe.

August   **2.** John Caldwell Calhoun to Monroe.

        3. John Quincy Adams to Monroe.

        4. Andrew Jackson to Monroe.

    15. William Harris Crawford to Monroe.

    18. Smith Thompson to Monroe.

    18. John Caldwell Calhoun to Monroe.

    18.   ''   ''

    22. Smith Thompson to Monroe.

    27. John Drayton to Monroe.

    28. Joseph Anderson to Monroe.

September   **5.** Smith Thompson to Monroe.

        6. Monroe to Thomas Jefferson.

        8. Alexander McRae to Monroe.

    15. Smith Thompson to Monroe.

    17. Monroe to Daniel Brent.

    19. John Quincy Adams to Daniel Brent.   [Extract.]

    21. William Wirt to Monroe.

    22. John Quincy Adams to Daniel Brent.   [Extract.]

    22. Smith Thompson to Monroe.

    25. Daniel Brent to Monroe.

    25. Cæsar Augustus Rodney to Monroe.

    29. Donatien Le Ray de Chaumont to Monroe.

    —. Monroe to Mrs. James Bowdoin.

October   **11.** William Wirt to Monroe.

    13. Benjamin Homans to Monroe.

    14. John Caldwell Calhoun to Monroe.

    29. Anonymous. Letter to Andrew Jackson. [Copy
        forwarded by Jackson to Monroe.]

November **13.** Andrew Jackson to Monroe.

          14.   "   "

          16. Richard Butler to Monroe.

          24. William Henry Winder to Monroe.

December   **3.** Richard Rush to Monroe.

          10. Charles Jared Ingersoll to Monroe. [Incomplete.]

          17. Richard Rush to Monroe.

          21. Countess Cabarrus to Monroe.

          24. Jonathan Roberts to Monroe.

          31. Monroe to Andrew Jackson.

          —. Joel Roberts Poinsett. Memorandum relating to the boundaries and geographical divisions of Buenos Ayres, Chile, and Peru.

1822.

January   **29.** Andrew Jackson to Monroe.

          29. Richard Rush to Monroe.

February   **4.** Albert Gallatin to Monroe.

          15. William Pinkney to Monroe.

          18. Daniel Wane to John Hollingsworth.

          20. Thomas Reilly to Cæsar Augustus Rodney.

          20. John Warner to Cæsar Augustus Rodney.

          24. John Hollingsworth to Cæsar Augustus Rodney.

March   **8.** W—— G—— D—— Worthington to Cæsar Augustus Rodney.

          12. Monroe to Jonathan Russell.

          14. Richard Rush to Monroe.

          18. Cæsar Augustus Rodney. Substance of address of minister to Buenos Ayres to the governor of that Republic.

          16. Cæsar Augustus Rodney to Monroe.

March 19. Andrew Jackson to Monroe.

29. Monroe to Robert S. Garnett.

29. Robert S. Garnett to Monroe.

—. Cæsar Augustus Rodney to Monroe.

April 2. Cæsar Augustus Rodney to Edward B. Jackson.

6. John Henry Eaton to Monroe.

8. Cæsar Augustus Rodney to Monroe.

29. J. Cox Barnet to Monroe.

—. Colonel Vincent. Memoir on the history of some islands in the Mediterranean, particularly Elba.

May 6. James Madison to Monroe.

10. Joel Roberts Poinsett to Monroe.

10. Monroe to James Madison.

11. James Wilkinson to Monroe.

18. Cæsar Augustus Rodney to Monroe.

18. James Madison to Monroe.

24. Richard Rush to Monroe.

30. Monroe to Andrew Jackson.

June 2. Cæsar Augustus Rodney to Monroe.

4. Charles Jared Ingersoll to Monroe.

5? Richard Rush. Notes on the art of building, equipping, arming, and navigating ships of war.

5. Richard Rush to Monroe.

8. Samuel Lewis Southard to Monroe.

13. Richard Rush to Monroe.

13. John Marshall to Monroe.

24. Joseph Story to Monroe.

25. William Noland to Monroe.

26. Charles Scott Todd to Monroe.

July   **3.**   Cæsar Augustus Rodney to Monroe.

         4.   ———— Mahy. Paper prohibiting John Warner from acting as commercial agent of the United States at Havana.

         7.   Abner Lacock to Monroe.

        11.   Francis C. Black to John Warner.

        12.   Henry Clay to Richard Mentor Johnson.

        13.   Cæsar Augustus Rodney to Monroe.

        20.   Joel Roberts Poinsett to Monroe.

        24.   Jonathan Roberts to Monroe.

August   **2.**   Cæsar Augustus Rodney to Monroe.

        3.   James Biddle to Monroe.

        13.   Joel Roberts Poinsett to Monroe.

        15.   Henry Dearborn to John Quincy Adams.

        22.   Alexander Macomb to John Caldwell Calhoun.

        25.   Monroe to James Madison.

        25.   Monroe to ————.

September   **7.**   Monroe to William Harris Crawford.

        14.   Richard Rush to Monroe.

        24.   James Madison to Monroe.

October   **1.**   Richard Rush to Monroe.

        1.   Cæsar Augustus Rodney to Monroe.

        5.   "   "

       12.

       20.   Richard Rush to Monroe.

       29.   Extract of a letter from a gentleman in Havana to his friend.

November   **1.**   La Baronne de Magrath to Monroe.

       13.   Albert Gallatin to Monroe.

November   **16.**   Cæsar Augustus Rodney to Monroe.

        29.   "   ''

December   **9.**   Levett Harris to Monroe.

        19.   Monroe to Charles Jared Ingersoll.

        20.   James Madison to Monroe.

        21.   William Taylor Barry to Monroe.

        —.   Monroe.   Notes relative to South American colonies.

        —.   William Wirt to Monroe.

        —.   William Johnson to Monroe.

1823.

January   **1.**   Charles Scott Todd to Monroe.

        27.   James Madison to Monroe.

        30.   Alexander Garrett.   Certificate as to valuation of land of Monroe.

        30.   Cæsar Augustus Rodney to Monroe.   [With inclosure.]

        30.   Richard Rush to Monroe.

        31.   Hugh Nelson, John Watson, and John Kelly. Opinion as to the value of certain land in Virginia belonging to Monroe.

February   **3.**   James Madison to Monroe.

        3.   William A. G. Dade to Monroe.

        5.   William P. Brobson to Cæsar Augustus Rodney.

        9.   Cæsar Augustus Rodney to Monroe.

        17.   "   ''

        21.   Thomas Jefferson to Monroe.

        26.   Richard Rush to Monroe.

        26.   Cæsar Augustus Rodney to Monroe.

March   **1.**   Albert Gallatin to Monroe.

March   8. Simon Bernaid to John Caldwell Calhoun.

11. Richaid Rush to Monioe.

16. Cæsai Augustus Rodney to Monroe.

25. Louisiana, Legislatuie.   Resolutions piotesting
against removal of regulai troops.

28. Thomas Jeffeison to Monioe.·

29.   "   "

April   6. Cæsar Augustus Rodney to Monroe.

6. Joel Robeits Poinsett to Monioe.

12. William B. Robeitson to Monroe.

14. Monioe to Geoige William Eiving.

16. José del Castillo to Joel Robeits Poinsett.

18. Geoige William Erving to Monioe.

24. Richaid Rush to Monroe.

24. John McLean to Monioe.

26. José del Castillo to Joel Roberts Poinsett.

29. John Tayloi to Monioe.

May   4. John Quincy Adams to Monroe.

5. Alexandei Hamilton to Monioe.

7. Joel Robeits Poinsett to Monioe.

10. John Quincy Adams to Monioe.

June   11. Thomas Jefferson to Monroe.

16. William Heniy Hariison to Monroe.

20. Richaid Rush to Monroe.

23. Thomas Jefferson to Monroe.

30. John McLean to Monioe.

July   2.   "   "

2. Richaid Rush to Monroe.

July   2. James Madison to Monroe.

4.   ''   ''

6.   ''

12. Paris Correspondent to Jeremy Bentham.

13. Richard Rush to Monroe.

14. John McLean to Monroe.

15. Caesar Augustus Rodney to Monroe.

21.   ''   ''

22. James Madison to Monroe.

26. John Andrew Graham to Monroe.

28. Hugh Nelson to Monroe.

29. James Madison to Monroe.

August   1. Richard Rush to Monroe.

3.   ''   ''

13. James Madison to Monroe.

22. John McLean to Monroe.

25. William Harris Crawford to Monroe.

26.   ''   ''

September 1. Monroe to John Caldwell Calhoun.

3. R. McC——— to ———.   [Last four pages.]

6. John Caldwell Calhoun to Monroe.

15. Richard Rush to Monroe.

25. George William Erving to William Harris Crawford.

October   6. Caesar Augustus Rodney to Monroe.

15. Monroe to Albert Gallatin.

21. James Madison to Monroe.

22. Richard Rush to Monroe.

October   **24.**   Thomas Jefferson to Monroe.

               26.   Albert Gallatin to Monroe.

               29.   John Caldwell Calhoun to Monroe.

               30.   James Madison to Monroe.

               30.   Daniel Sheldon, jr., to John Quincy Adams.

               31.   James Madison to Monroe.

November   **4.**   "   "

               13.   Joseph M. White to Monroe.

December   **1.**   Richard Rush to Monroe.

               2.   Monroe. Portion, of 7th annual message, relating to the Cumberland road.

               6.   James Madison to Monroe.

               9.   John Marshall to Monroe.   ·

               17.   Mariano Cubi y Soles to Monroe.

               23.   James G. King to Rufus King. [Extract.]

               23.   James Madison to Monroe.

               26.   James Madison to Monroe.

1824.

January   **6.**   Richard Rush to Monroe.

               10.   James Brown to Monroe.

               16.   Andrew Jackson to Monroe.

               23.   James Brown to Monroe.

               28.   Richard Rush to Monroe.

February   **3.**   "   "

               3.   James Lloyd to Monroe.

               5.   James Madison to Monroe.

               5.   Thomas Jefferson to Monroe.

               7.   Alexander McRae to Monroe.

February   8.   Caesar Augustus Rodney to Monroe.   [Incomplete.]

10.   "   "

13.   James Brown to Monroe.

15.   "   "

18.   Rufus King to Samuel Lewis Southard.

19.   Richard Rush to Monroe.

20.   James Brown to Monroe.

23.   Richard Rush to Monroe.

27.   Andrew Jackson to Monroe.

28.   "   "

—.   Monroe's Secretary to ———.

March   14.   Richard Rush to Monroe.

16.   "   "

16.   Andrew Jackson to Monroe.

27.   Thomas Jefferson to Monroe.

April   9.   Andrew Jackson to Monroe.

10.   James Madison to Monroe.

10.   Andrew Jackson to Monroe.

15.   George William Erving to Monroe.

15.   James Brown to Monroe.

24.   Abner Lacock to Monroe.

May   5.   John Henry Eaton to Monroe.

8.   "   "

17.   Monroe to William Harris Crawford.

18.   Walter Lowrie to Monroe.

20.   Joel Roberts Poinsett to Monroe.

20.   Andrew Jackson to Monroe.

28.   Nicholas Biddle to Monroe.

May	30.	James Brown to Monroe.
June	5.	Richard Rush to Monroe.
	12.	James Brown to Monroe.
	21.	Monroe to the members of the Cabinet.
	29.	L—— A—— Tarascon to Monroe.
July	3.	Hyde de Neuville to Monroe.
	12.	James Brown to Monroe.
	14.	Thomas Leiper to Thomas Jefferson.
	18.	Thomas Jefferson to Monroe.
	18.	Richard Rush to Monroe.
	19.	William Henry Harrison to Monroe.
	19.	Joel Roberts Poinsett to Monroe.
	22.	Thomas Jefferson to Monroe.
	29.	William Wirt to Monroe. [Incomplete.]
	31.	Richard Rush to John Quincy Adams.
August	2.	" "
	3.	Joseph Anderson to Monroe.
	5.	James Madison to Monroe.
	14.	Charles Jared Ingersoll to Monroe.
	17.	Joseph Anderson to Monroe.
	18.	Lafayette to Monroe.
	19.	Hugh Nelson to Monroe.
	29.	" '
September	11.	John Caldwell Calhoun to Monroe.
	13.	Richard Rush to Monroe.
	17.	" "
	22.	William Wirt to Monroe.
	25.	Monroe to Samuel Smith.

September **26.** William Noland to Monroe.

26. James Brown to Monroe.

27. Monroe to William Wirt.

October **20.** John Caldwell Calhoun to Monroe.

28.   ''   ''

28. James Brown to Monroe.

November **15.** John Adams to Monroe.

23 James Brown to Monroe.

—. Lafayette to Monroe.

December **11.** Monroe to Thomas Jefferson.

12. Richard Rush to Monroe.

13. John Marshall to Monroe.

15. Thomas Jefferson to Monroe.

16. James Madison to Monroe.

—. Cæsar Augustus Rodney. Notes on treaties of nations to protect neutrals.

1825.

January **20.** James Brown to Monroe.

23. Monroe to John Quincy Adams.

February **3.** John Quincy Adams to Monroe.

15. Samuel Whittlesey Dana to Monroe.

March **7.** John Marshall to Monroe.

10. Monroe to John Marshall.

29. Joel Roberts Poinsett to Monroe.

May **23.** Monroe to Edward Everett.

July **3.** Monroe to Andrew Jackson.

13. John Marshall to Monroe.

22. Samuel Lewis Southard to Monroe.

August **30.**   ''   ''

September **7.** Henry Unwin Addington to Monroe.

12. Samuel Lewis Southard to Monroe.

18. Monroe to Henry Unwin Addington.

October **8.** Christopher Hughes to Monroe.

November **20.** Daniel Bentalou to Monroe. [With inclosure.]

25. Henry Wheaton to Monroe.

December **1.**   "   "

14.

19. Henry Lee to Monroe.

—. Monroe to Jacob Brown.

—. Monroe to John Caldwell Calhoun.

—. Monroe to Samuel Lewis Southard.

—. Monroe. Answers to interrogatories in relation to Commodore David Porter.

—. Monroe to —— [respecting Porter].

—. Monroe to ——.

—. Monroe. Notes respecting Commodore Porter.

1826.

January **15.** Monroe to Thomas Jefferson.

20. Samuel Lewis Southard to Monroe.

21. Thomas Jefferson to Monroe.

February **13.** Monroe to Thomas Jefferson.

22. Thomas Jefferson to Monroe.

23. James Brown to Monroe.

March **8.** Thomas Jefferson to Monroe.

April **15.**   "   "

23. Daniel Pope Cook to Monroe.

27. Monroe to Daniel Pope Cook.

May   **1.** William Wirt to Monroe.

             8. Monroe to Tench Ringgold.

July   **17.** Benjamin Watkins Leigh to Monroe.

             20. John McLean to Monroe.

             24. Samuel Lewis Southard to Monroe.

             30. John Marshall to Monroe.

August   **6.** John McLean to Monroe.

             —. James Madison.   Notes on publication of the jour-
                    nals and correspondence of the Continental
                    Congress.

September   **20.** James Madison to Monroe.

             30. James Brown to Monroe.

October   **6.** James Barbour to Monroe.

             20. Monroe to James Barbour.

             31. John McLean to Monroe.

November   **3.**

             5. Samuel Lewis Southard to Monroe.

             11. John McLean to Monroe.

             —. Monroe to William Thornton.

December   **3.** John McLean to Monroe.

             5. Monroe.   Extract from the *U. S. Telegraph*

             —. Monroe to Richard Jones.

             —. Benjamin Vaughan.   Notes on Monroe's first mis-
                    sion to France.

1827.

January   **9.** James Madison to Monroe.

             26. Monroe to Hugh Lawson White.

             29. Hugh Lawson White to Monroe.

             —. Monroe to James McIlhany.

February	1.	John McLean to Monroe.
	4.	Samuel Lewis Southard to Monroe
	5.	George Bomford to Monroe.
	9.	Monroe to Hugh Lawson White.
	21.	Hugh Lawson White to Monroe.
	30.	[sic] John Caldwell Calhoun to Monroe.
March	18.	James Madison to Monroe. [Copy by Dolly Madison.]
	19.	James Madison to Monroe.
April	16.	Henry Wheaton to Monroe.
	25.	Monroe to ———.
	—.	Monroe to Henry Wheaton.
May	27.	James Madison to Monroe.
June	5.	Albert Gallatin? to Monroe. [Copy by Dolly Madison.]
	26.	James Madison to Monroe.
	28.	James Brown to Monroe.
July	9.	James Madison to Monroe.
	27.	Samuel Lewis Southard to Monroe.
September	24.	James Madison to Monroe. [Circular, copy by Dolly Madison.]
October	7.	Thomas Sidney Jesup to Monroe.
	9.	Monroe to John McLean.
	10.	Tench Ringgold to Monroe.
	10.	" "
	12.	
	29.	James Madison to Monroe.
November	1.	George Bomford to Monroe.
	15.	John McLean to Monroe.

November   25.   Monroe to Charles Jared Ingersoll.

December   2.   James Madison to Monroe.

                 5.   Monroe to John McLean.

                 9.   John Caldwell Calhoun to Monroe.

                 9.   ''   '

                10.   Monroe to Hugh Mercer.

                11.   James Madison to Monroe.

                15.   John Taliaferro to Monroe.

                16.   Monroe to John Caldwell Calhoun.

                16.   Samuel Lewis Southard to Monroe.

                19.   John McLean to Monroe.

                20.   John Quincy Adams to Monroe.

                22.   John Caldwell Calhoun to Monroe.

                28.   Monroe to John Caldwell Calhoun.

                28.   John McLean to Monroe.

                —.   Monroe. Notes of Correspondence with Henry
                      Wheaton.

                —.   Monroe to ———.

                —.   Anonymous to Walter Lowrie.   [Copy by Monroe.]

1828.

January   3.   John Caldwell Calhoun to Monroe.

                 7.   Monroe to Edmund Tyler, J—— M—— Smith,
                      T—— C—— Quinlan, and T—— Maund.

                 9.   John McLean to Monroe.

                13.   Hugh Mercer to Monroe.

                25.   Monroe to John McLean.

                28.   John McLean to Monroe.

February   7.   Joel Roberts Poinsett to Monroe.

February   **11.** Samuel Lewis Southard to Monroe.

             21. Monroe to Francis John Brooke.

March   **1.** Samuel Delucenna Ingham to Monroe.

             3. Monroe to Francis John Brooke.

             3. George Graham to Monroe.

             7. Francis John Brooke to Monroe.

             7. John Caldwell Calhoun to Monroe.

             13. George Graham to Monroe.

             16. Monroe to John Caldwell Calhoun.

             18. Monroe to John McLean.

             21. John McLean to Monroe.

             23. David Michie to Monroe.

             24. John McLean to Monroe.

             30. Henry Lee to Monroe.

             —. Monroe to ———.

April   **13.** Edward Livingston to Monroe.

             20. Monroe to Edward Livingston.

             23. Monroe to Henry Lee.

             —. John Caldwell Calhoun to Monroe.

May   **1.** John Caldwell Calhoun to Monroe.

             1. Thomas Mann Randolph, sr., to Monroe.

             1. William Short to Monroe.

             6. Henry Banks to Monroe.

             24. Henry Lee to Monroe.

June   **3.** James Madison to Monroe.

             16.   ‘   ‘‘

             23. Monroe to Henry Lee.

July   **3.**   “   “

July	10.	John Caldwell Calhoun to Monroe.
August	2.	John McLean to Monroe.
	4.	Monroe to John Caldwell Calhoun.
	11.	James Madison to Monroe.
	12.	John McLean to Monroe.
	17.	Monroe to John McLean.
September	13.	John McLean to Monroe.
	19.	'' ''
October	20.	Monroe to Charles Jared Ingersoll.
	20.	Joseph C. Cabell to Monroe.
	24.	Monroe to William Wirt.
November	21.	Richard Rush to Monroe.
	24.	Monroe to John McLean.
December	3.	Monroe to Richard Rush.
	17.	Monroe to John Quincy Adams.
	18.	Monroe to Lord Brougham.
	21.	Richard Rush to Monroe.
	—.	Monroe to Andrew Jackson.
	—.	Monroe to ———.

1829.

January	4.	Samuel L. Gouveneur to John Quincy Adams.
	7.	Monroe to John Caldwell Calhoun.
	17.	John Quincy Adams to Samuel L. Gouverneur.
	24.	Hugh Nelson to Monroe.
	27.	Monroe to Hugh Nelson.
March	12.	James Barbour to Monroe.
	26.	James Madison to Monroe.
April	2.	Samuel M. Edwards to Monroe.

April   **4.** John McLean to Monroe.

        6. Monroe to Samuel M. Edwards.

        14. Samuel M. Edwards to Monroe.

        14. Samuel M. Edwards and others to Monroe.

        14. Charles Jared Ingersoll to Monroe.

        17. Monroe to Samuel Lewis Southard.

May   **1.** James Madison to Monroe.

        2. Monroe to Lafayette.

        26. Barbé Marbois to Monroe.

        29. Monroe to Peter Stephen Du Ponceau.

June   **17.** Lafayette to Monroe.

        24. Monroe to Barbé Marbois.

September **15.** James Madison to Monroe.

October   **29.** Lafayette to Monroe.

November **12.** Hugh Nelson to Monroe.

        23. John McLean to Monroe.

December **10.** de Survilliers (Joseph Bonaparte) to Monroe.

        10? de Survilliers to Marquand.

        10? de Survilliers.   "Notice sur la Cession de la Loui-
                siane."

        15. Vincent Gerry to Monroe.

        21. Monroe to Joseph Bonaparte.

1830.

January   **21.** Samuel L. Gouverneur to Monroe.

May   **17.** John Caldwell Calhoun to Monroe.

        18. James Madison to Monroe.

        19. Monroe to John Caldwell Calhoun.

        21.   "   "

        26.

May   **26.** John Caldwell Calhoun to Monroe.

June   **28.** Hugh Nelson to Monroe.

July   **2.** Monroe to James Madison.

                 5. William Harris Crawford to Monroe.

August   **1.** Monroe to Samuel L. Gouverneur.

                 8. Monroe to William Harris Crawford.

September   **8.** Lafayette to Monroe.

October   **19.** Benjamin Vaughan to Monroe.

November   **26.** I—— K—— Cowperthwaite and William Osborn to Monroe.

December   **4.** Monroe to ————.

                 15. James Madison to Monroe.

                 15. Hugh Nelson to Monroe.

                 27. John Sergeant to Samuel L. Gouverneur.

                 —. Monroe to I—— K—— Cowperthwaite.

                 —. Monroe.   Memoranda respecting Andrew Jackson's conduct in the Seminole war.

1831.

January   **10.** John Quincy Adams to Monroe.

                 11. John Caldwell Calhoun to Monroe.

                 11.   "   "

                 14. Charles Fenton Mercer to Monroe.

                 21. John Caldwell Calhoun to Monroe.

                 24. Monroe to John Caldwell Calhoun.

                 25. Monroe to John Quincy Adams.

                 27. Monroe to John Caldwell Calhoun.

                 27. John Caldwell Calhoun to Monroe.

                 27.   "   "

January	29.	John Quincy Adams to Monroe.
	31.	William Wirt to Monroe.
February	1.	Samuel Lewis Southard to Monroe.
	4.	Monroe to William Wirt.
	4.	John Caldwell Calhoun to Monroe.
	8.	Monroe to Samuel Lewis Southard.
	14.	Monroe to John Quincy Adams.
	16.	John Caldwell Calhoun to Monroe.
	—.	Monroe to John Caldwell Calhoun.
	—.	Monroe to a Committee of Tammany Hall.
	—.	Monroe to the Governor of Virginia.
	18.	John Quincy Adams to Monroe.
March	11.	Monroe to John Quincy Adams.
	21.	Abner Smith Lipscomb and others to Monroe.
	29.	Samuel Lewis Southard to Samuel L. Gouverneur.
April	4.	Committee of New Orleans to Monroe.
	11.	Monroe to James Madison.
	16.	John Caldwell Calhoun to Samuel L. Gouverneur.
	16?	John Caldwell Calhoun. "Extracts from Mr. Crawford's letter to me relating to Mr. Monroe."
	4.	Hugh Nelson to Monroe.
	21.	James Madison to Monroe.
May	28.	Dutee J. Pearce to Monroe.
June	3.	John Rhea to Monroe.
	3.	
	11.	Samuel L. Gouverneur to William Wirt.
	13.	Tench Ringgold to Samuel L. Gouverneur.

June   16. William Wirt to Samuel L. Gouverneur.

          18.   "   "

          19. Monroe.   Denunciation of the insinuations of John
              Rhea.

          27. William Wirt to Samuel L. Gouverneur.

          —. Anonymous.   Explanation of the causes which
              induced the authority to Mi. Calhoun to publish
              Mr. Monroe's coirespondence with General Jack-
              son respecting the Seminole wai.

          —. Monroe to ———.

July   14. John Caldwell Calhoun to Samuel L. Gouveineur.

          19. Samuel L. Gouverneur to John Quincy Adams.

August   1. John McLean to Samuel L. Gouverneur.

           6. Tench Ringgold to Samuel L. Gouverneur.

           8. John Caldwell Calhoun to Samuel L. Gouverneur.

          17. William Wirt to Samuel L. Gouverneui.

          18. John Caldwell Calhoun to Samuel L. Gouverneur.

          30. John Quincy Adams to Samuel L. Gouveineur.

September 3. Samuel Lewis Southard to Samuel L. Gouverneur.

          19. John McLean to Samuel L. Gouveineur.

          25.   "   "

1832.

January   6. John Young Mason to James Madison.

February 13. John Caldwell Calhoun to Samuel L. Gouverneur.

March   4.   "   "

          12. John Young Mason to James Madison.

June   14. John Caldwell Calhoun to Samuel L. Gouverneur.

1835.

June   11. Anonymous to Samuel L. Gouverneur.

32067—04——8

1839.

February   **13.**   Barnabas Bates to Samuel L. Gouverneur.

—.   Monroe to John Quincy Adams.

—.   Monroe to ————.

—.   Monroe to ————.

—.   Monroe to ————.

—.   Monroe to ————.

—.   Monroe.   "Substance of correspondence with General Jackson—sent to Washington."

—.   Cipher key.

O